Praise for *The Enterprise Data Catalog*

This book is a much-needed and refreshing addition to the data catalog landscape. Ole masterfully combines industry and practical experience with information and library science concepts to provide data catalog implementers with essential techniques for delivering a superior data discovery experience for their organization.

— *Juan Sequeda, Ph.D., Principal scientist and head of AI Lab, data.world*

Ole Olesen-Bagneux's book helps enterprise organizations navigate the complex data landscape with higher precision than ever before. It highlights the tremendous opportunity we have to harvest the full value of investing in data through an enterprise data search engine. Ole provides the magical missing piece that enables data-driven organizations to reach their full potential. This book is a must-read for all IT professionals, data authorities, and data enthusiasts.

— *Ann Fogelgren, Chief Information Officer, GN Group*

For too long the information science and data management communities have been far apart. Dr. Olesen-Bagneux's groundbreaking work clearly demonstrates the vital necessity of bringing these communities together toward realizing the full potential of data assets. The fresh perspectives developed in his book show us the way forward for innovation both in practice and in the study of data systems that reflect the human context of data work.

— *George Fletcher, Professor in the Data and Artificial Intelligence Cluster, Eindhoven University of Technology*

Information science techniques have always been used to retrieve information that meets people's informational needs. What if we applied these techniques to data catalogs to discover strategic data for an organization? In this book, Ole wisely demonstrates chapter by chapter how this is possible.

— *Fabiola Aparecida Vizentim, Librarian, ontologist,*
data architect, IA Biblio BR Group

Making data accessible is a challenge for most data-driven enterprises. In his book, Ole addresses a key component: the search for data. I find it especially inspiring and shocking how easily we can use thousands of years of knowledge from librarians and apply it to our modern data and metadata problems, including difficult topics such as data lineage. Impressive book.

— *Tomas Kratky, Founder and CEO, Manta Software*

I highly recommend *The Enterprise Data Catalog* for anyone who wants to improve their data management skills and make better data-driven decisions. It's a comprehensive guide that will help you understand and implement best practices for data cataloging, discovery, and governance. Ole has done an outstanding job.

— *Ravit Jain, Founder and host of* The Ravit Show,
data science evangelist

By applying library and information science principles to an area largely driven by software engineering disciplines, this book offers fresh perspectives and directly applicable advice to data novices and veterans alike.

— *Nikolaj Agerbo Sabinsky,*
Principal consultant, Sabinsky Consult

A foundational and comprehensive book that will benefit practitioners and strategists alike. Theory and methodology from library and information science is used to understand both the problems faced and the solutions to be applied, illuminating in an engaging way the tasks of organization, curation, discovery, and management of data to achieve organizational success. Data catalogs are poised to become the essential enterprise application, and this book is likely to become an essential guidebook to implementing and ensuring their success.

— *Deb Seys, Senior director,*
Learning and Communities, Alation

Brillant introduction to data catalogs. Well-written and sharp,
this book presents both conceptual background and practical tools for
how to develop and implement enterprise data catalogs.

— *Jens-Erik Mai, Professor of Information,*
University of Copenhagen

Olesen-Bagneux's ideas and use of techniques from the world of library science
bring data catalogs to life with improved access to information,
a better user experience, and stronger collaboration.

— *Mark McLellan, Product strategy, Rowbot.io*

Ole Olesen-Bagneux offers a unique point of view about data catalogs.
Lucid and full of insights, his book is destined to become
the definitive guide to data catalog evaluation and implementation.

— *Jeffrey Tyzzer, Senior solution architect, Starburst*

The Enterprise Data Catalog provides data practitioners and data curators with the critical
skills they need to organize and search for data in meaningful ways. Ole makes clear the
foundational role of metadata in information discovery, and in the process highlights the
importance of information science professionals in modern data environments.

— *Susannah Barnes, Data intelligence program lead, Alation*

With more and more technologies promising to "solve the data problem," *The Enterprise
Data Catalog* provides a fresh, much-needed, vendor-agnostic explanation of why and
how data catalogs must work. In simple, non-salesy terms, this book shows that
simply cataloging data in the right way can restore our collective ability to connect
and create shared understanding across enterprises. A great guide for anyone
trying to tame the enterprise data wilderness and unlock its potential.

— *Mark D. Kitson, Data strategy and management consultant,*
independent, Global Fortune 500 firms

The Enterprise Data Catalog

Improve Data Discovery, Ensure Data Governance, and Enable Innovation

Ole Olesen-Bagneux

Beijing · Boston · Farnham · Sebastopol · Tokyo   

The Enterprise Data Catalog

by Ole Olesen-Bagneux

Copyright © 2023 Ole Olesen-Bagneux. All rights reserved.

Published by O'Reilly Media, Inc., 1005 Gravenstein Highway North, Sebastopol, CA 95472.

O'Reilly books may be purchased for educational, business, or sales promotional use. Online editions are also available for most titles (*https://oreilly.com*). For more information, contact our corporate/institutional sales department: 800-998-9938 or *corporate@oreilly.com*.

Acquisitions Editors: Aaron Black & Jess Haberman	**Indexer:** Judith McConville
Development Editor: Rita Fernando	**Interior Designer:** David Futato
Production Editors: Clare Laylock & Katherine Tozer	**Cover Designer:** Karen Montgomery
Copyeditor: nSight, Inc.	**Illustrator:** Kate Dullea
Proofreader: Tim Stewart	

February 2023:   First Edition

Revision History for the First Edition

2023-02-15:   First Release

See *https://oreilly.com/catalog/errata.csp?isbn=9781492098713* for release details.

978-1-492-09871-3

[LSI]

Table of Contents

Part II.   Democratizing Data with a Data Catalog

Foreword

When I began focusing on data cataloging in the mid-2010s, the world of data analytics had reached an inflection point. The great modern data infrastructure projects, centered on *data lakes* and usually tied to internal Hadoop clusters, had reached a level of maturity. The technical architecture was in place. The promise of innovation and value creation, however, which had been the initial argument in favor of massive spending in the infrastructures of organizations, had hardly borne fruit beyond a few use cases driven by enthused pioneering teams.

I feel this relative failure has its roots more in the governance of these new transverse infrastructures than in the technology per se. These failures manifested themselves in two opposing ways.

In some cases, the lack of governance caused data lakes to morph into data swamps— enormous storage spaces containing data whose content and origin were unknown to everyone, and which nobody knew how to use.

In other cases, the deployment of sophisticated governance tools locked the data within complex and bureaucratic procedures, thus inhibiting the agility and experimentation that are needed at the heart of innovation.

As a result, organizations began migrating (or creating) their analytic infrastructures to the cloud (the state of the art of cloud solutions has massively improved since the middle of the 2010s) and rethinking how best to manage the huge volumes of data they needed to exploit.

There is, of course, plenty to say about modern data architectures, but I am particularly interested in the data management aspect, which has existed for longer than one might think.

As far back as ancient Greece, we have been manipulating vast volumes of information. Since then, we have been confronted with the challenges of organizing information to make it useful within the best possible conditions.

Callimachus was an ancient Greek poet, scholar, and librarian of the Great Library of Alexandria. He probably took over from Zenodotus, himself a successor of Demetrius Phalereus, as the head of the Great Library. Demetrius, considered to be one of the greatest Greek thinkers, had been the creator and architect of the Great Library and had supervised the collection of tens of thousands of papyrus scrolls. It's quite likely that, as with most premodern erudites, Demetrius had a phenomenal memory that probably helped him recall each and every book in the library and their locations and thus allowed him to answer the questions of his colleagues and researchers who frequented the library. This overview knowledge naturally died with him, leaving Callimachus with a problem that any data manager today can relate to when the team that created the data lake moves on to new pastures—staff turnover in data teams can be very high. Demetrius was essentially a living index and search engine, and without him, library patrons had no way to quickly identify what materials they needed to access, and no way to quickly find them. They would need to browse the library to find what they needed.

I feel Callimachus had been confronted with the same challenges modern organizations face with their data lakes today.

Callimachus thought of a solution whose principles are still valid today. He built a complete registry of all the papyrus scrolls in the library and arranged them in alphabetical order so as to index the content. These registries, named *Pinakes*, of which a few fragments were found, contained biographical information on the authors as well as bibliographic descriptions of the scrolls: title, opening words, number of lines on each roll, literary genre/discipline, and subject. The authors within a given category and the titles from the same author were arranged in alphabetical order, building upon Aristotle's categorical practices but applied on a much larger scale.

Essentially, he developed a system for metadata that provided information about each roll without having to actually read the scroll. He then consigned and organized the metadata in an indexed registry. In effect, he cataloged the content of the library. I imagine he also defined a number of procedures that ensured the upkeep of the catalog as the library added new books over time. In the predigital age, this must have been a colossal endeavor.

Today, as was the case in the times of Alexandrian greatness, metadata management, organization, and indexation are key to managing information and enabling its access to the greatest number of users. Information distribution specialists know this very well. It's the case for media libraries obviously, but also for video streaming platforms (can you imagine Netflix without information indexed to its content?), ecommerce websites, image banks, market data brokers, or even the internet. Google is, after all, a vast collection, production, and structured metadata indexation tool. Information distribution specialists understand that metadata is as important as the data itself. Indeed, it is the metadata that enables their clients to choose the content they wish to use and it is the metadata that enables data to generate value. We all experience this when we browse our own hard drives. The file system is nothing other than a rather minimalist metadata management arrangement, without which it would become impossible to make sense of the thousands of documents we have stored.

The central role of metadata is something traditional organizations sometimes have a hard time grasping. The art of enterprise metadata management was long considered repetitive and superfluous when, in my opinion, it is one of the most important levers to maximize fully the potential of the new data architectures. To be blunt, I don't believe it is possible to deploy a large-scale data strategy without a suitably structured and maintained catalog, which is the reason why I set sail on the Zeenea adventure a few years ago.

When I first met Ole a couple of years ago, I was impressed by the fluidity of his thoughts on the role of the enterprise data catalog and also by the convergence of our convictions on the topic. Back then, I was still espousing a pragmatic approach to the data catalog as a search and exploration tool, and meeting somebody with the same vision helped further strengthen my own convictions.

The strength of his book, *The Enterprise Data Catalog*, goes beyond placing *discovery* at the heart of the data catalog. It also provides a complete and structured guide to its deployment in the organization. He provides a clear road map for organizations looking to make the most of their data investments and also provides a great source of inspiration for solutions providers, such as myself.

There is a lot of honesty and intelligence in these pages, and whatever your role currently is in the deployment of your enterprise data strategy, this book will radically alter your perception of the importance of metadata and the data catalog in your strategy and will ultimately open new horizons on the road to success.

— Guillaume Bodet,
CPTO and Cofounder of Zeenea

Preface

"This simply can't be all there is to a data catalog. What does it really do?"

About five years ago, I sat alone in the office among 20 empty desks. My company had shut off the air-conditioning to go green, so I was uncomfortably warm on top of being perplexed by the bunch of white papers, both printed and on my laptop, that were sitting in front of me. The papers explained a new technology called a data catalog. As an enterprise architect, I had been asked to implement a data catalog for our company. But first, I had to understand it.

The papers I was looking at described cool, advanced features: column-based data lineage, graph visualizations of ontologies, and workflows to access virtualized data. Useful. Mesmerizing, really. But what was the overall point of a data catalog? I was sweating, physically and mentally, trying to draw upon my experiences to figure out the potential of this new technology.

I have a BA, MA, and PhD in library and information science (LIS). I have taught LIS in university courses and been to conferences all over the world. I've seen a lot of things in this field, both good and bad. During my first job in pharma, senior management regularly called me late at night because inspections from the authorities were going haywire. The inspectors were asking them a multitude of questions: What was the temperature of this tube, in that machine, in June 1992? Where is the proof that the fermentation tank was cleaned according to the standard operating procedure (SOP)? When the data managers searched and couldn't answer, they called my team—the Records and Information Management team.

We employed our searching superpowers to find the information they needed. We were adept with our queries, used intuition and creativity to plan our moves, and drew on our knowledge to guide our search. We were able to do this because we had one guiding principle: *How you organize data defines how you can search it*. Because we knew how the data was organized, we knew ways to begin searching, modifying how we searched, broadening, changing focus, excluding hits, and finding the information we needed. Sometimes this was easy, and sometimes it was hard, but we would get there every time.

This guiding principle has followed me throughout my career. I have cataloged furniture, weapons, human tissue, a lot of paper, and massive amounts of data. I know how to structure and operate a physical card catalog in a library. I know records and information management systems with both physical and digital storage. We both stored and cataloged data on premises, and then, later, in the cloud. Throughout everything I experienced, I saw that if you have a poorly organized data landscape, searching for the information you need will be a terrible experience. You will have to guess where to search and what to query. If your data is logically and systematically organized, however, you will know exactly where to look and what to query. It will be a much better experience.

The idea that how you organize data defines how you search for it is reflected in our web habits as well. We never really think about how we search it anymore; it's so intuitive. At work, within our company's IT landscape, it can be a different story. We search in vain—companies hardly know their own data, let alone how it is processed. Data is undiscoverable and unmanageable. If only we had an enterprise search engine…

On that hot summer day, alone in the empty office, surrounded by physical papers and dozens of open PDFs on my laptop, it suddenly hit me.

"This data catalog has the potential to become a search engine for companies! We are finally getting an engine that will be able to do for companies what search engines have done for the web. The data catalog is a search engine!"

That realization led to another a few years down the road. All of the papers I read that fateful day, along with all of the documentation that followed it, focused on explaining the complex features that are in data catalogs. They did not explain the data catalog itself and how it could revolutionize how we organize and search data. Nowhere has anyone talked about the future of the data catalog as an enterprise search engine. That realization has brought us to the book you are reading today.

Who Should Read This Book

Although I had the epiphany about the potential of a data catalog and it was crystal clear in my head, I was then faced with the battle of explaining the features to the important stakeholders of my company. Although I knew they would see the benefits of this tool if they only took the time to understand it, they were simply not interested, nor did they have time to study it. I had to come up with a way to reach them.

I went back to the idea of using the data catalog as an enterprise search engine. So, I asked myself, "What are people searching for? What would a data scientist be searching for? A data protection officer? A chief information security officer?"

I decided to build demonstrations of the most vital data catalog features into small stories about specific stakeholders. Each slide deck had one central picture: a minimalist search bar with the company's logo above it. I would explain the information need of a specific stakeholder, show the search in the search bar, reveal the result, then close with how the results could be used. In this way, I showed simple searches, complex searches, how to browse back and forth in the lineage of data, up and down in domains, and relationally in the graph that depicted our company. It had the same content as my previous demonstrations, but this time, it was explained from a stakeholder point of view: a specific person who was searching for something specific. And that worked.

The stakeholders not only got interested, but they also got excited. They now wanted the data catalog, because they understood that this tool was not just a collection of fancy features for data geeks. No, this tool was something way more fundamental: the data catalog could help them search and find the data they were looking for. I explained that, implemented with care, a data catalog has relevance for many of the employees in a company. This approach worked for me and my colleagues, and I hope that it will work for you and yours as well.

At the end of the day, we are all searching for something. And we search all the time. The only thing is, at work, it is very difficult to search for whatever we are trying to find. And we take that for granted, as something that we must just accept.

I'm assuming you're reading this book because you're involved with planning to implement a data catalog, improve an existing one, sunset it, or simply trying to understand what kind of technology a data catalog is: what it does, how it should be used, and if it can help you in a certain way. You might be part of the offices of the legal counsel, chief data officer, data protection officer, or chief information officer. You might be a data engineer, data scientist, or data manager, or you might be part of the data governance team. If you are, then this book will help you understand what a data catalog is and how it will enable you to find exactly what you are searching for.

However, you may also be a data catalog provider. In my book, I put forward a vision for the future of data catalogs, which you could benefit from when planning the future development of your data catalog technology.

Navigating This Book

This book is both a practical guide for understanding, implementing, and using data catalogs in the present, *and* a vision for a company search engine of the future.

This is my vision: I foresee that the data catalog will evolve into a company search engine. My vision is first and foremost about memory and recollection of knowledge in companies. I envision a mental state where company employees are no longer suffering from collective amnesia but instead remember the knowledge they have accumulated over the years and have that knowledge close at hand—just a search away.

Unlike many visions in the world of data and tech, my vision does not evangelize a specific technology or concept, such as chatbots or artificial intelligence, for example. You may call it a technology-agnostic vision, aside from the fact that I see the data catalog tech category evolve into company search engines. I will let the data catalog providers compete over what kind of technologies will best serve such a future. But I do consider knowledge graph databases as hard to ignore in this context, either as part of or supporting the data catalog as it crests the ultimate searchability of data and knowledge in companies.

With this book, you will also learn a principle: *how you organize data defines how you can search it*. For example, I deep dive into how you design data domains and subdomains, and this is because the better you have structured your data domains, the better you can search them. The same goes for glossaries and all other metadata that you apply in your data catalog. It's a matter of making all the data in your company as searchable as possible.

And this opens endless possibilities of discovery. No one can predict how these possibilities will unfold, but the better the data is organized, the more impact it can have when you search for it.

Where does this principle come from? Not data management. In fact, this book is written not just from a data management perspective, but also from an LIS perspective. LIS has studied and innovated catalogs for over three centuries, so we should capitalize on it. A fundamental reality in LIS is that how you organize data, information, and knowledge defines how you can search it.

This book has three parts:

- Part I, "Organizing Data So You Can Search for It"
- Part II, "Democratizing Data with a Data Catalog"
- Part III, "Envisioning the Future of Data Catalogs"

In Part I, you will learn the basics of organizing data in domains, creating glossaries, and searching the data catalog. You will encounter a fruitful alternative to how domains are understood in domain-driven design, and you will be equipped with an understanding of concepts, mechanics, and methods that will allow you to search data catalogs with maximum effect.

In Part II, we take a closer look at how the data catalog is a contributor to data democratization—the fact that more and more employees can discover, access, and manage data independently of a small, central team. Accordingly, I discuss how all the stakeholders and end users of the data catalog can use it for data governance and data analytics.

In Part III, I put forward my vision of the company search engine. Drawing on LIS, I suggest that data catalogs will not only focus on data but on knowledge, and that data will be grouped in larger chunks, to be understood as *works*, like an artistic or intellectual expression. The company search engine will be able to search for knowledge and works, and establish a true company memory.

Conventions Used in This Book

The following typographical conventions are used in this book:

Italic
: Indicates new terms, URLs, email addresses, filenames, and file extensions.

`Constant width`
: Used for program listings, as well as within paragraphs to refer to program elements such as variable or function names, databases, data types, environment variables, statements, and keywords.

This element signifies a tip or suggestion.

This element signifies a general note.

This element indicates a warning or caution.

O'Reilly Online Learning

 For more than 40 years, *O'Reilly Media* has provided technology and business training, knowledge, and insight to help companies succeed.

Our unique network of experts and innovators share their knowledge and expertise through books, articles, and our online learning platform. O'Reilly's online learning platform gives you on-demand access to live training courses, in-depth learning paths, interactive coding environments, and a vast collection of text and video from O'Reilly and 200+ other publishers. For more information, visit *https://oreilly.com*.

How to Contact Us

Please address comments and questions concerning this book to the publisher:

O'Reilly Media, Inc.
1005 Gravenstein Highway North
Sebastopol, CA 95472
800-998-9938 (in the United States or Canada)
707-829-0515 (international or local)
707-829-0104 (fax)

We have a web page for this book, where we list errata, examples, and any additional information. You can access this page at *https://oreil.ly/the_enterprise_data_catalog*.

Email *bookquestions@oreilly.com* to comment or ask technical questions about this book.

For news and information about our books and courses, visit *https://oreilly.com*.

Find us on LinkedIn: *https://linkedin.com/company/oreilly-media*.

Follow us on Twitter: *https://twitter.com/oreillymedia*.

Watch us on YouTube: *https://youtube.com/oreillymedia*.

Acknowledgments

I am fortunate to have written a book that some of the brightest minds in data have reviewed, commented on, and enabled the refinement of. This book has been improved by data practitioners, university professors, industrial researchers, entrepreneurs, and some of the most brilliant CEOs of the data catalog tech space. I have done my best to make this book an enjoyable, solid read, and if you find it to be so, it's first and foremost thanks to the generous, clever people that have helped me along the way.

I am thankful to the technical reviewers: Jack Andersen, associate professor, University of Copenhagen; Vinoo Ganesh, CEO and founder of Efficiently; Ron Itelman, principal, Clarkston Consulting; Niklas Lagersson, head of enterprise architecture, GN Store Nord; and Jessica Talisman, senior manager, taxonomy, at System1. With their thoughtful, precise comments, based on academic, practical, and technical expertise, my book turned out better than I could have hoped.

My good friend Juan Sequeda, principal scientist at data.world, has conversed with me about data, knowledge, and data catalogs in chats on LinkedIn, Zoom, and on the phone from the subway, in cars, at the airport, and from his home. He is a teacher and a true intellectual academic, with a nonstop thinking brain and a big heart. Juan, meeting you and Professor George Fletcher in Paris was so, so fun and mind-stimulating!

At the Data Innovation Summit 2022 in Stockholm, I met Luc Legardeur, CEO of Zeenea, and Petter Tønnessen, head of Nordic operations, both from Zeenea. We met later again in Paris with the CEO of Zeenea, Guillaume Bodet. Discussing world politics, European history, data, and my book in the cafés of Paris was extraordinary.

Having a world-leading expert in data lineage like Tomas Kratky, founder and CEO of MANTA—the Nikola Tesla of data!—reading my manuscript was challenging, and it improved my book. Thanks, Tomas, it was so generous of you.

Thanks to Prukalpa Sankar, the cofounder of Atlan, for commenting on and reviewing my manuscript. Every company should activate their metadata, and data catalogs must help do exactly that!

Thanks to Shinji Kim, the founder and CEO of Select Star, and Inna Tokarev Sela, the founder and CEO of illumex, for reaching out and discussing their first-class technology and my book.

Shirshanka Das, cofounder and CEO of Acryl Data, took the time to explain in detail the wonders of streaming-based data catalogs and provided helpful feedback on my manuscript—thank you, Shirshanka.

Awais Ahsan, senior vice president, and Mitesh Shah, vice president, both from Alation—we have had good exchanges on my manuscript, more to come. Thank you so much!

Eric Broda, senior technology executive, helped detail the relation between data catalogs and data mesh; thank you!

I have also received good feedback from Piethein Strengholt, Andy Petrella, Xavier de Boisredon, Benjamin Rogojan, Chad Sanderson, Girish Kurup, Fabiola Aparecida Vizentim, and Elie Perelman.

Thanks to the podcasters for having me on! Scott Hirleman on *Data Mesh Radio* (*https://oreil.ly/-oQMG*), Loris Marini on *Discovering Data* (*https://oreil.ly/kdQIv*),

Winfried Adalbert Etzel on *MetaDAMA* (*https://oreil.ly/aw7HE*), Juan Sequeda (yes, him again!) and Tim Gasper on *Catalog and Cocktails* (*https://oreil.ly/lRTlD*), Joe Reis and Matt Housley on *Monday Morning Data Chat* (*https://oreil.ly/GpeaU*), and Jocelyn Byrne Houle on *Software Engineering Daily* (*https://oreil.ly/yFQQt*). All of you educate so many people—keep it up!

Thanks to the editorial team at O'Reilly: my acquisitions editors, Aaron Black, Jess Haberman, and Jon Hassell; my development editor, Rita Fernando; and my production editors, Clare Laylock and Katherine Tozer. You shaped, refined, and completed my ideas and turned them into a book. Working with my editors has been one of the most professional experiences in my career; O'Reilly is lucky to have them. They are gifted, friendly people.

Finally, my family. To my bright, beautiful wife, Christina Eriksen, you are the love of my life, and my children, Lili and Louis, you are truly wonderful kids. Thank you, all of you, for giving me the time to write this book.

And if I didn't mention *you*, it's not that you are forgotten! Thank you!

PART I

Organizing Data So You Can Search for It

This first part of the book is about the most fundamental reality in library and information science: how you organize data defines how you can search it. It's a reality that automatically enforces itself in all sorts of inventories, repositories, lookup tools, and search engines, and also in data catalogs.

In Chapter 1, "Introduction to Data Catalogs", I will discuss what a data catalog is from a high-level perspective: the core functionality of a data catalog, its technological components, who uses it and who maintains it, and the benefits of a data catalog.

Then, in Chapter 2, "Organize Data: Design a Robust Architecture for Search", I deep dive into how you should design your data catalog. I will explain how to build stable logic structures that will be able to contain data in a logical way over a long period of time.

Chapter 3, "Understand Search: Concepts, Features, and Mechanics", introduces you to search. The main capability of data catalogs is search, and in this chapter, you get the necessary insight to understand how search works.

Finally, Chapter 4, "Apply Search: From Simple to Advanced Patterns", makes everything come together. You know how a data catalog works, you know how to organize data, you know how search works, and now, in this chapter, you will see how you can apply search. You will truly see that how you organize data defines how you can search it.

CHAPTER 1

Introduction to Data Catalogs

In this chapter, you'll learn how a data catalog works, who uses them, and why. First, we'll go over the core functionalities of a data catalog and how it creates an overview of your organization's IT landscape, how the data is organized, and how it makes searching for your data easy. Search is often underutilized and undervalued as part of a data catalog, which is a huge detriment to data catalogs. As such, we'll talk about your data catalog as a search engine that will unlock the potential for success.

In this chapter, you'll also learn about the benefits of a data catalog in an organization: a data catalog improves data discoverability, subsequently ensuring data governance and enhancing data-driven innovation. Moreover, you'll learn about how to set up a data discovery team and you'll learn who the users of your data catalog are. I'll wrap up this chapter by explaining the roles and responsibilities in the data catalog.

OK, off we go.

The Core Functionality of a Data Catalog

At its core, a data catalog is an organized inventory of the data in your company. That's it.

The data catalog provides an overview at a metadata level only, and thus no actual data values are exposed. This is the great advantage of a data catalog: you can let everyone see everything without fear of exposing confidential or sensitive data. In Figure 1-1, you can see a high-level description of a data catalog.

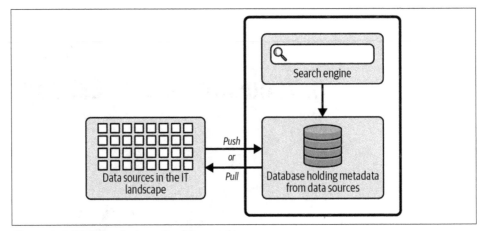

Figure 1-1. High-level view of a data catalog

A data catalog is basically a database with metadata that has been pushed or pulled from data sources in the IT landscape of a given company. The data catalog also has a search engine inside it that allows you to search the metadata collected from the data sources. A data catalog will almost always have a lot more features, but Figure 1-1 illustrates the necessary core components. And in this book, I argue that the search capability is the single most important feature of data catalogs.

In this section, we will discuss the three key features of the data catalog, namely that it creates an overview of the data in your IT landscape, it organizes your data, and it allows you to search your data. Let's take a brief look at how data catalogs do this.

With a data catalog, your entire organization is given the ability to see the data it has. Used correctly, that transparency can be very useful. For example, data scientists will no longer spend half their time searching for data, and they will have a much better overview of data that can really deliver value. Imagine the possibilities. They could be using their newfound time to analyze that data and discover insights that could lead the enterprise to developing better products!

Create an Overview of the IT Landscape

Creating an overview of your IT landscape involves finding and displaying all the data sources in it, along with listing the people or roles attached to it.

A data catalog can pull metadata with a built-in crawler that scans your IT landscape. Alternatively, it can get metadata pushed to it by having your data systems report metadata to your catalog. We will discuss push and pull in more detail in Chapters 2 and 6.

The IT landscape that is reflected in your data catalog will get business terminology added to it as "tags"—terms that are created in the data catalog and organized in glossaries. We will discuss glossary terms in Chapter 2 and how to search with them in Chapter 3. Besides glossary terms, you can also enhance your data catalog's assets with metadata, complete with additional descriptions, classifications, and more.

Furthermore, a data catalog has various roles and permissions built in, such as data steward, data owner (data catalogs have different role type names), and other roles that all carry out specific tasks in the data catalog. I will describe those roles for you at the end of this chapter.

Once you have pulled/pushed your IT landscape and assigned selected terms, other metadata, and roles to it, it's searchable in the catalog.

No employee can see all the data in the IT landscape. Even more confusing: no employee can see what data others can see. Basically, no one knows about all the data in the IT landscape: it's opaque.[1] This reality is also referred to as *data silos*.

Data silos emerge when several groups of employees work with their own data in their own systems, isolated and unaware of the data in the rest of the organization.

This state—the data siloed state—is the root cause of an immense set of problems in many organizations, which the data catalog addresses and ultimately solves. These problems include data analytics applied to data lacking quality, incomplete datasets, and data missing security and sensitivity labels.

This perspective can also be flipped: data silos are connected, but no one can see it or knows how. This makes the data siloed state even more dangerous, but as you will see, capabilities in the data catalog can help map the data.

In the data catalog, it's the complete opposite situation of the IT landscape itself. Everything in the data catalog is visible to all employees. Everyone can see everything—at the metadata level. And accordingly, all employees can get an idea of all the data in their company, based on that metadata. They are mindful and aware of the data outside their own, now past, data silo.

---

1 If your IT department is very well organized, a few employees may have a very high-level overview of all types of data via tools such as a configuration management database (CMDB) and an Active Directory (AD). Remember that Figure 1-1 illustrates the states for the vast majority of employees in the company, not the select few in an IT department.

The more the data catalog expands, the more everyone can see. If this makes you think that a data catalog holds remarkable potential, you're not wrong—and you will discover the magnitude of that potential in this book.

Based on my experience, I suggest you organize data in a data catalog in the following way.

Organize Data

As a data catalog crawls the IT landscape, it organizes the metadata for data entities within the landscape as assets pertaining to a data source and stores them in domains. However, you play a big part in this: you must design the domains and part of the metadata that the assets are assigned. And keep in mind that most data catalogs offer automation of this process—it should not be a manual task to add metadata to assets.

What is an asset? An asset is an entity of data that exists in your IT landscape. It could be a file, folder, or table, stored in a data source such as an application or database, etc. Assets are, for example, documents in a data lake, SQL tables in a database, and so on. When the data catalog collects metadata about the asset, whether by push or pull methods, it obtains information such as the asset's name, creation date, owner, column name, schema name, filename, and folder structure. Overall, the collected metadata depends on the data source and the data that sits in it. You must add metadata to the asset beyond what was populated by the push/pull operation. We'll talk more about this in Chapter 5.

And so what is a data source? Simply put, a data source refers to where the data that is being exposed at a metadata level in the data catalog comes from. It can be an IT system, application, or platform, but it can also be a spreadsheet. In the context of this book, the type of data source is irrelevant because all data sources can be treated in the same way.

You must be aware that data catalogs that crawl IT landscapes (i.e., that pull, not push) come with standard connectors to only a selected set of data sources. So, not everything will be crawlable by the data catalog. Therefore, sometimes, useful assets have to be manually entered, by stewards or other subject-matter experts.

A domain is a group of assets that logically belong together. These assets may stem from one or more data sources. For example, a domain with finance data may both have analytics data sources and budget data sources. It is critical to define your domains with care because they should be intuitive for employees outside that domain—and they should be intriguing to explore for those employees—a data catalog is an initial step toward breaking data silos!

So far, data catalogs have only been described in the data-management literature. In that literature, the understanding of domains refers solely to domain-driven design (DDD), as an attempt to push DDD thinking into the mapping of data in the entire IT landscape. In this book, you'll find domain thinking extended to the century-long tradition of domain studies in information science. This will provide you with a deeper, more functional understanding of domains than in normal data-management literature—you'll find all this in Chapter 2.

Now that you have a better idea of how assets, data sources, and domains work, let's look at a few examples of how they all fit together. Figure 1-2 shows a table in a database (also known as a data source, in a data catalog) and how it's visible as an asset in the data catalog.

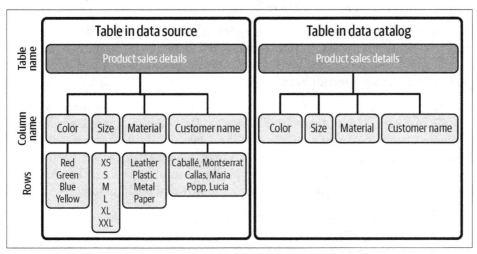

Figure 1-2. Table in a data source and how it's visible as an asset in the data catalog

As you can see to the right side of the figure, no values are included in the asset in the data catalog. In this case, sensitive data—customer names—is not visible in the data catalog as it is in the data source. In the data catalog, only the column name is displayed. In this way, everyone can see everything in the data catalog. It's the actual values in, for example, tables that have prevented a complete overview of data in your company. With the data catalog, those days are over, and you can ignite data-driven innovation and enhance data governance.

Dataset names, column names, and other metadata visible in the data catalog can also contain sensitive or confidential data. When you push or pull metadata into your data catalog, methods must be in place to make sure that such metadata is not visible to the users of the data catalog.

You can add metadata to your asset—in this case, a table—both at the table level and for each column. Every piece of metadata added to your asset will inscribe it with context relevant to the knowledge universe of your organization. This will make your asset more searchable. We'll talk more about how to organize it in Chapter 2 and how to search for it in Chapter 3.

Furthermore, it's important to understand that assets should be organized into vertical, horizontal, and relational structures, as can be seen in Figure 1-3 and more exhaustively in Figure 2-12 in Chapter 2.

Vertical organization enables you to pinpoint exactly what kind of data your asset represents. This is achieved through domains and subdomains. In the Product Sales Details asset in Figure 1-3, the vertical organization specifies which part of the company the data comes from; for example, finance.

The horizontal organization of assets allows you to display how the asset moves in your IT landscape. This is done with *data lineage*. Data lineage depicts how data travels from system to system and, ideally, how the data is transformed as it travels. In the Product Sales Details in Figure 1-3, lineage would, for example, display that the dataset resides in a database and that it is used in a business intelligence (BI) report, indicated by an arrow to the right of the asset, pointing toward the BI report.

The relational organization of assets depicts how parts of any asset relates to other assets and, if done correctly, can render these relations in a graph database. In the Product Sales Details assets in Figure 1-3, the relational organization of the Size column could, for example, be related to other volume metrics data in other assets, e.g., from manufacture data, referring to machine volume capacity, and so on.

All together, a fully organized table asset in a data catalog is depicted in Figure 1-3.

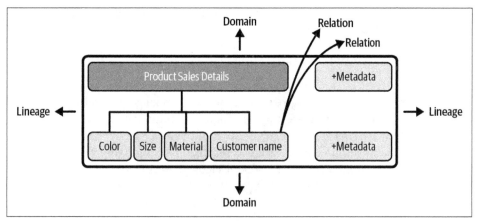

Figure 1-3. A fully organized asset in a data catalog

Once your assets have been organized into neat vertical, horizontal, and relational structures (for examples of this, check out Chapter 2), you might be tempted to think that your job is done and you no longer need to work on your magical data catalog. That is not the case! You should not consider a data catalog to be a repository that only needs to be organized once. You should always be open to reorganizing assets and improving the metadata quality and coverage. Not only will it ensure things are neat and tidy, but it will optimize your assets for search.

Accordingly, let's take a first look at searching a data catalog.

Enable Search of Company Data

Search is one of the key functionalities of a data catalog. It is often treated as just a feature, but it can be so much more than that if you make it the driving factor of your data catalog strategy. Think of your data catalog as a search engine, the same kind of search engine that you'd use to peruse the web. A data catalog and a web search engine are similar in that they both crawl and index their landscapes and allow you to search that landscape. The main difference is that while a web search engine covers the web as a landscape, a data catalog covers your organization's IT landscape.

So, what does it look like when you treat your data catalog as a search engine? Let's take a look at one in action.

Throughout this book, we'll be looking at the data catalog of Hugin & Munin. Hugin & Munin is a fictitious Scandinavian architecture company that specializes in sustainable construction that uses wood from forests close to their building sites.

The Hugin & Munin data catalog revolves around organizing data and searching for it. Figure 1-4 shows the interface for the Hugin & Munin catalog. The search bar allows you to enter terms to do a regular search of the data catalog, but you can click the Advanced button to do a more detailed search. The magnifying glass allows you to use the browser function and a pile of books icon gives you access to the glossaries. Note that this looks very similar to most popular web search engines.

Figure 1-4. The data catalog frontend in Hugin & Munin

Let's look at how you might use this data catalog. Say that you are an employee at Hugin & Munin and you overhear a group of people in the canteen during lunch.[2] They talk about this clever data scientist named Kris, mentioning that he's an asset steward for some SQL table assets in your company's data catalog (you'll learn about asset stewards later in this chapter; right now it's not important). Such SQL tables could be useful in the projects you are currently working on. Before you can ask the group about how to contact Kris, they've collected their food and left the canteen. Back at your desk, you search the data catalog as depicted in Figure 1-5.

---

2 In some European countries, it is common for companies to maintain a small cafeteria or snack bar on their premises where employees can buy food and eat together.

Figure 1-5. First search for Kris

That search returns an enormous number of hits. The Kris you're looking for is most likely in there somewhere, but there are too many imprecise hits to go through them all. Instead, you narrow the search to look only for asset stewards, as depicted in Figure 1-6.

Figure 1-6. Second search for Kris

That's definitely better, but there are still so many different people called Kris that you need another way to find what you are searching for. Perhaps you can search for the term "data science" in the central glossary? You give it a go, as illustrated in Figure 1-7.

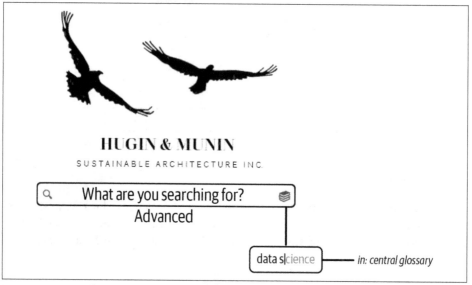

Figure 1-7. Searching for the glossary term "data science"

And you receive tons of hits. But wait! You can filter on asset types, and you remember the group of people mentioning SQL tables. You filter on SQL tables tagged with the term "data science." And then, you get the idea of ranking those hits alphabetically by the asset steward—yes! There we go, you see the assets associated with Kris displayed on the screen! They're all nicely arranged; each column in the SQL tables has been given descriptions and glossary terms. You would definitely like to take a look at this data, so you push the "request access" button that pings Kris for your request. You succeeded. Then, you realize that you could have just used an advanced search like in Figure 1-8.

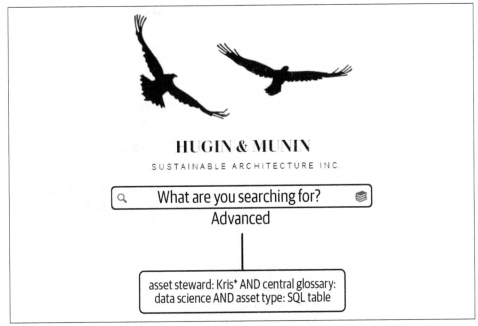

Figure 1-8. Advanced search for the exact information you need

You've got a glimpse of how search works in the example, but search is described in full depth in Chapter 3. The more searchable your data is, the more you enable the one big benefit of a data catalog: data discovery.

Data Discovery

A data catalog enables all employees to search all data in their company. Searching and actually finding data is called *data discovery*, and that's what a data catalog is all about.

Nevertheless, data discovery is rarely thought of as searching *for* data, but often as searching *in* data, in databases, to find new insights about customers, products, etc.

Searching *for* data can be haphazard conversations with colleagues, by memory, or it can be structured, meaning that searching for data takes place in a formalized manner in a solution designed for the purpose of searching for data,[3] for example, a data catalog. The difference between searching for data and searching in data may strike you as not very important—but it is! And we will discuss it in detail in Chapter 3.

---

3 G. G. Chowdhury, *Introduction to Modern Information Retrieval* (New York: Neal-Schuman Publishers, 2010), chaps. 1 and 2.

Put simply, *data discovery* begins with discovering that certain data exists at all, not what's inside it. Once you get your data catalog up and running, you will exponentially accelerate data discovery *in* data, because the preceding search *for* data is remarkably more effective with a data catalog than without it.

Data discovery *for* data, in a data catalog, has a distinct target state: *ambient findability*. This term was coined by Peter Morville in the first literature that shed an intellectual light on the powerful search engines on the web that arose in 1995–2005:

> Ambient findability describes a fast emerging world where we can find anyone or anything from anywhere at anytime.[4]

Today, data catalogs are emerging as the company equivalent of web search engines. And data catalogs, too, should strive for ambient findability. That's how smooth data discovery *for* data must be: in your data catalog, you should be able to find anyone or anything from anywhere at any time—in your company.

 Ambient findability is completely unrelated to how you search *in* data. Searching in data is so persnickety and subtle that an entire field has evolved out of it: data science. I discuss this extensively in Chapter 3.

Data discovery in a data catalog serves two purposes:

- Data analytics
- Data governance

Data analytics supported by a data catalog is pretty simple: data scientists—analysts and similar profiles—all need data. Without a unified, global overview of all data in your company, these highly paid employees just work with the data they happen to know—in their data silo—and not the best-fit data for what they want to do. You can change that with a data catalog and create a complete overview of all the data in your company. This means that data-driven innovation can accelerate and deliver substantially more value.

Data governance supported by a data catalog has many advantages, and I'll discuss these in depth in Chapter 4. The most important one is the capability to classify all data in your IT landscape both in terms of sensitivity and confidentiality. This will be of great value for your data protection officer (DPO) and your chief information security officer (CISO)—indeed, for your entire company. A data catalog applies rules

---

4 Peter Morville, *Ambient Findability: What We Find Changes Who We Become* (Sebastopol, CA: O'Reilly, 2005), 6.

to its pull/push capability so that all its assets are automatically assigned a sensitivity classification and a confidentiality classification. You can take a look in Chapter 2 about this for more details. For now, just remember that the power of automated classification of sensitivity and confidentiality directly on your IT landscape is a bedazzling feature that won't be difficult to sell.

Data catalogs are also used by people who do not have many tech skills; I discuss them in the following as everyday end users.

The Data Discovery Team

A data management job—including managing a data catalog—is not the job of one person alone. Rather, it is the work of an entire team to implement, maintain, and promote the usage of the data catalog across your organization. Although you could call this your data catalog team, I encourage you to call this your data discovery team instead. This tells everyone not just what technology you use, but on what capability you deliver, which is data discovery.

Data discovery teams can focus solely on data catalogs or more widely on all metadata repositories. You should push for the latter: preferably, the data discovery team owns and curates all metadata repositories like the CMDB (configuration management database), data sharing agreement system, etc. that describe everything within the IT landscape. In this way, it can promote data discovery from the totality of sources where these are exposed at a metadata level.

Who works in a data discovery team? You can divide data discovery team members into two basic profiles: architects, for frontend, and engineers, for backend.

Data Architects

A data architect provides advice to all end users of the data catalog and works in the data catalog frontend. Data architects provide counseling in specific contexts of organizing data and searching it. They have the ultimate responsibility for the map of the IT landscape in logical domains, and they oversee the expansion of the map according to that structure. Data architects are responsible for monitoring the lifecycle of assets. In that context, they ensure that no assets are left without relevant roles assigned to them and that the retention times for the assets are correctly managed.

A time-consuming task for data architects is to educate end users to be independent and work with only a minimum of support from the data discovery team itself. Accordingly, data architects design and teach courses in the data catalog about how to organize data and search data:

Organize data

This includes topics that will make end users capable of adding and managing their data sources in the catalog themselves, such as:

- Pushing/pulling data sources into the data catalog. This includes identifying the data source, attaching all the roles to it, and using rules for automated classification of data. (We'll discuss roles and responsibilities later in this chapter.)

- Designing and applying automated processes of adding metadata to assets. For example, descriptions and terminology from the glossaries, either via usage of APIs or via built-in functions in the frontend of the data catalog.

- Creating and managing glossary terms.

Search data

This includes teaching end users how to search for data using techniques such as:

- Simple search, what it does, and how you can use it. Most likely, simple search won't be as smooth and intuitive as search engines on the web, but there are ways to get close to that state.

- Browsing in all dimensions, that is, vertical in domains and subdomains, horizontal in data lineage, and relational in associative structures connected to your asset.

- The information retrieval query language (IRQL) behind the advanced search feature and what this query language allows and is unfit for, compared to simple search and browse.

Furthermore, two additional tasks can be assigned to the data architects, in setups where the data discovery team is oriented more toward data governance:

Perform second-level support across the company under inspections from authorities

If the data catalog is used in a highly regulated industry, it can be a powerful tool to answer complex questions from inspectors. Questions asked by an inspecting authority are typically subject to short deadlines—they need fast answers. Each department should be capable of searching its own data in the data catalog and answering questions during inspections. But if they are unable to find what they are searching for, the data catalog steward functions as a second-level support, capable of searching absolutely anything in the data catalog.

Execute or design queries to perform all legal holds across the company
> Legal holds compel a company not to delete data, called electronically stored information (ESI), by the US Federal Rules of Civil Procedure. In order to do so, data needs to be identified and blocked from deletion. Accordingly, a data catalog can play a vital role in correctly addressing and enforcing legal holds.

Finally, the data architects maintain the most conceptual overview of the data catalog, called the *metamodel*. You can see an example of a metamodel in Figure 1-9. The metamodel is the model that provides an overview of all entities in the data catalog. The metamodel also includes all relations between the entities. For example, departments have people, perform processes, and are supported by technology. Basically, the metamodel defines how you can physically structure your data catalog, based on conceptual metadata structures.

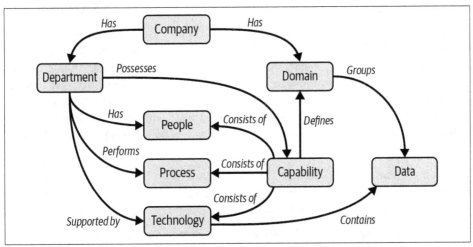

Figure 1-9. Example of a metamodel in a data catalog

Consider the metamodel in Figure 1-9. In this hypothetical example, a *company* has two entities, *departments* and *domains*. Departments and domains are not alike, as we will discuss in Chapter 2. A *department* has *people*, performs a *process*, and is supported by *technology*. Furthermore, a *department* possesses a *capability*. *Capability* defines a *domain*, and *domain* groups the *data* that the *technology* contains.

At a first glance, a metamodel may provoke dizziness. But the metamodel is there to provide the best possible structure for the data that is represented in the data catalog. It organizes data into its most relevant dimensions so that it is as easy to search for as possible.

Metamodels differ substantially from provider to provider, from very simple metamodels to very complex ones. Simple metamodels are not less desirable than complex ones; they both have pros and cons. Simple metamodels make your data catalog easy to implement but can show weakness in terms of the refinement of organizing your data catalog in the long run. Complex metamodels provide the latter but can be unduly intricate and difficult to implement.

 Knowledge graph–based data catalogs have flexible metamodels. The metamodel in such data catalogs can be visualized, expanded, and searched without limits. This technology is likely to gain more influence on the data catalog market, as it very powerfully caters to the most important feature in a data catalog: search.

Data Engineers

Data engineers work in the backend of the data catalog and assist the data architect on more technical issues for organizing data, searching it, and providing access to it.

The data catalog engineer supports data architects and end users in setting up the actual push/pulls of data sources into the data catalog. This may include usage of an API to curate assets with metadata, lineage, or the like. They oversee the functionality of rules that classify and profile data when pulling/pushing data into the data catalog, and they create additional rules for classifying data. The engineer merely ensures that the rules work, based on feedback and conversations with the data architect, who gathers knowledge from conversations with end users and employees from CISO and DPO functions.

The data catalog engineer ensures that data catalog search activity is appropriately logged and measured so that the data catalog counselor has the best chance of improving the search features of the catalog.

Once end users discover data that they want to access, the data catalog engineer is involved in providing guidance and practical help if needed. More simple access requests may simply include that the access requester is created as an end user in/of the data source. But if the data source has to be used in a software context, where the data in the source is to be exposed or processed, then the complexity of providing access to the source increases. There are three ways to get data from the data source to the one requesting it: read-only data stores (RDSs), APIs, and streaming.

Finally, the data catalog engineer manages the data catalog environments on test, dev, and prod (if more than one environment exists), including all security aspects and backend management of user profiles.

Data Discovery Team Setup

The data discovery team can be set up in three different ways, focusing on supporting:

- Data governance
- Chief data officer (CDO)
- Data analytics

I discuss them in depth in Chapter 5. But briefly, the benefits of each way can be described as follows:

Data governance ensures that data is managed in accordance with regulations and standards. It also focuses on data quality aspects, ownership, etc. The advantage of placing the data discovery team in a data governance part of the company is that it leads to better data compliance and efficiency of the operational backbone. You will ensure that confidential and sensitive data is protected. Nevertheless, if such an approach is used, a data catalog should merely be considered an expense to ensure data governance, and not as the key component it is intended to be for data-driven innovation.

Having a *CDO* responsible for the data discovery team is the ideal, but also a rare setup for a data catalog. In this case, the data discovery team is a staff function for the CDO. The CDO writes and puts into action the executive data strategy of a company and should therefore have a full overview of all data at hand. In such a case, the executive data strategy is based on empirical facts, and outcomes are measurable.

Placing the data catalog in a *data analytics* business unit puts the data catalog directly into action where it delivers the most value: innovation. However, the risk of this setup is a lack of control. Without firm data governance, the data catalog can risk exposing confidential data or processing sensitive data in a way that is a liability to your company or in a way data subjects have not consented to. It can also create difficulties for data quality, which is a time-consuming effort that an energized team seeking results could be tempted to neglect.

End-User Roles and Responsibilities

End users of a data catalog fall into three categories:

- Data analytics end users
- Governance end users
- Everyday (efficiency) end users

Data analytics end users search the data catalog for data sources to inform innovation, and their data discovery does not end in the data catalog when they search for data. Data discovery *for* data leads to data discovery and data exploration *in* data, as we will discuss in Chapter 3. Data analytics end users should be considered the most important end users of the catalog, as they will deliver the return on investment (ROI) for the data catalog. They do so by innovating new offerings to customers, based on data they have searched, found, analyzed, and used for business opportunities and growth.

Governance end users primarily search the data catalog for either confidential data or sensitive data—or both—in order to protect that data. They do so both as the catalog expands with new data sources (I discuss this in Chapter 5) and on an ongoing basis, when performing risk assessments and during daily operations. They also use the data catalog to get a more managed approach to who can see what data in the organization. The data catalog will enable them to increase the data governance of the company, but an ROI is more difficult to document in comparison with data analytics end users.

Everyday end users are likely to become the most substantial group of end users in the future. You can go to Chapter 8 to check what that future looks like in detail. At the point where the data catalog truly evolves to become a company search engine, employees are going to use it for everyday information needs. These are expressed with simple searches and are aimed at reports, strategy papers, SOPs, and basic access to systems. Currently, everyday end users of a data catalog are not a very big group. But you can plan your implementation in such a way that everyday end users become larger in numbers, with the effect that the data catalog gets more traction in your company. I discuss this in Chapter 5.

All end users have one or more of the following roles and responsibilities in the data catalog:

Data source owner
> The data source owner is also known as simply the system owner or data custodian in traditional data management.

Domain owner
> A domain owner manages a specific collection of assets. The domain owner ultimately defines which assets belong in the domain and who should have the different roles in the domain.

Domain steward
> A domain steward takes on more practical tasks such as conducting interviews with upcoming data source owners, managing the domain architecture, and providing access to data.

Asset owner
> The asset owner is the owner of the data in the data source. Typically, data ownership spans multiple data sources (as data ownership spans multiple systems), and it can also in rare cases span multiple domains. It is the asset owner that grants access to data upon request.

Asset steward
> An asset steward has expertise on a particular subset of assets (an entire data source or parts of data sources) in a domain.

Term owner
> Term owners typically own a large subpart of glossaries related to one or more domains in the data catalog.

Term steward
> Term stewards are responsible for managing term lifecycles. (See Chapter 7 for details.)

Everyday end user
> Everyday end users are able to search the data catalog and request data from asset owners.

 Collectively, the end users of a data catalog constitute a social network. If they can work in groups independently of the data discovery team, the data catalog will provide the most value. See Chapter 5 for details on this.

Summary

You have now gotten the first impression of a data catalog. This unique tool represents a powerful step for your company toward better, more secure use of your data.

Here are the key takeaways of the chapter:

- Data catalogs are organized in domains that contain assets. The assets are metadata representations of data in source systems. The assets have either been pulled (crawled) or pushed into the data catalog.

- Organized to its maximum capacity, your data catalog will be able to cater to a completely free and flexible search, from simple search, to various ways of browsing, to advanced search.

- The strategic benefit of a data catalog is data discovery. For the first time, companies are now able to discover all their data in a structured and endless way.

- Data discovery serves data-driven innovation and data governance. Innovation is the most important and is the reason why data catalogs emerged in the first place. Data governance, on the other hand, is not as profitable but is important in its own right—it secures data.

- Accordingly, end user types fall into categories of data analytics, governance, and everyday users. The end users can have different and even multiple roles and responsibilities in the data catalog.

- Instead of having a "data catalog team," promote the capability that such a team delivers by calling it a "data discovery team." The data discovery team consists of architects working in the frontend of the data catalog and engineers in the backend.
- There are three possible setups for data discovery teams:
  — The team can be focused on data governance, with the risk of losing the innovative potential of the data catalog.
  — The team can be focused on innovation, with the risk of compromising data governance.
  — The best possible setup is as a staff function for a CDO, who should take every strategic decision based on the data that's actually in the company, be it for innovative or governance purposes.

In the next chapter, we'll talk about how you organize data in the data catalog.

CHAPTER 2

Organize Data: Design a Robust Architecture for Search

You can't discover and map the entire world in a day. Likewise, you can't discover and map the IT landscape of your organization in one go. As you discovered in Chapter 1, the effectiveness of a data catalog is heavily dependent on how well it is structured and managed—this impacts how well it can be searched. Although it may sound straightforward, organizing your assets and their metadata isn't simple. You will have to ask yourself: what is the most logical way to group data? What's the most relevant metadata for my data assets? How do my data assets relate? Can they relate in multiple ways? And what is the interplay between how confidential data is, and how sensitive it is?

In this chapter, we'll go through these kinds of questions and walk through the process of gathering and organizing the assets in a data catalog. We'll begin with how to organize domains, proceed to a brief discussion of how you populate the domains with data, and end with how to organize your data once it's represented in the data catalog.

Let's first have a look at how you organize domains.

Organizing Domains in the Data Catalog

As I discussed in Chapter 1, a domain groups assets that logically belong together. Accordingly, the first thing you need to do is to create your domains. You do not need to create them all at once, just the ones you need to begin to push/pull your first data sources. Once you have that, you can then organize the assets within the domains. We'll discuss that later.

But what does organizing the domains really mean in the context of a data catalog? In a data catalog, it is up to the domain owners to define what assets go into their domain. In the following subsections, I will provide you with a guide to architect domains.

Domain Architecture in a Data Catalog

The task of organizing your domains can be a messy one. Without a reference architecture for your domains, you might not even know where to start.

Imagine a standard classification tree, like the one you can see in Figure 2-1. It has a root that leads to separated subcategories, which again can have further subcategories and so on. It's a structure that can expand as needed in breadth and depth.

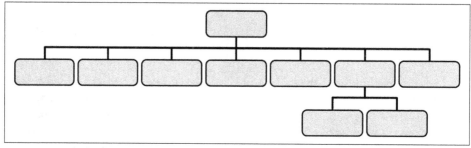

Figure 2-1. Classification tree

That is how you should organize the domains. But how?

Have no fear. I have created a domain architecture for data catalogs to get you started and group your data sources in a logical, systematic way. You can see it in Figure 2-2. With this architecture in hand, you get a framework that will allow you to keep a firm hand on the tiller when you organize your domains. This is the hands-on guide to group all your data sources in a logical, systematic way.

The top level of Figure 2-2 is the data catalog main entry. The *main entry* is the root of all the domains and a logical starting point. Think of it as your entire catalog: everything is subdivided from here. It's not recommended (and in many data catalogs impossible) to have multiple main entries, for two reasons:

- Each asset from each data source can be stored in only one place. This means that all levels need to relate to one top level, as it all constitutes subdivisions of one body of data: the data of your organization.

- Your data discovery team needs complete control of the entire data catalog, as I discussed in Chapter 1. Therefore, you need one top level, from which all roles and responsibilities are assigned in the lower levels.

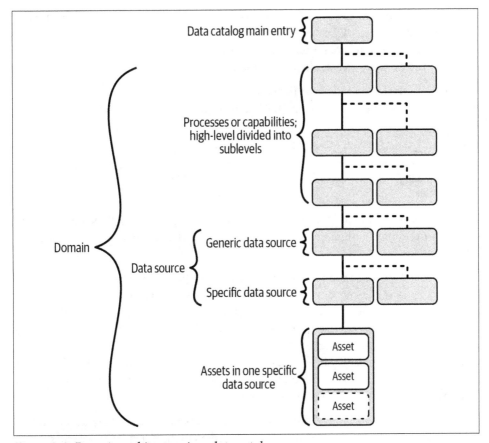

Figure 2-2. Domain architecture in a data catalog

Before I talk about the various layers of the data catalog architecture, you first need to have a deeper understanding of what is meant by *domain*.

Understanding Domains

If you want to understand what a domain is, two fields can deliver answers:

- Domain-driven design
- Library and information science

It's domain-driven design (DDD) that is dominant in data management—and subsequently most known in a data catalog context. But as you will see later in this subsection, DDD is not a completely proper fit when you architect domains in the data catalog. And so first, I will briefly describe the understanding of a *domain* in DDD and information science.

DDD emerged in the early 2000s and was formulated in the book *Domain-Driven Design* by Eric Evans.[1] DDD enables software engineers to better understand and cater to the context to create usable, logical software. In DDD, software design is driven by the domain it's created for—domain-driven design.

Remember: DDD is intended for the creation of software. You can see just how intermingled domain and software is in DDD, in this quote from Eric Evans:

> Every software program relates to some activity or interest of its user. That subject area to which the user applies the program is the *domain* of the software.... To create software that is valuably involved in users' activities, a development team must bring to bear a body of knowledge related to those activities.... Models are tools for grappling with this....[2]

So, in DDD, understanding a domain is about creating software that models users' activities or interests—taking into account the knowledge those activities/interests rely on.

These days, DDD is becoming relevant for a new purpose, this time not for software, but for data. It is the movement known as *data mesh*, which has applied DDD for data. Data mesh suggests a way to create scalable data infrastructure that allows for analytical data to spread faster, and easier, in a federated governance model where each business unit is responsible for storing, exposing, and providing access to its data. I discuss data mesh architecture in more depth in Chapter 6, as well as how I see this architecture in relation to a data catalog. For now, you only need to know that data mesh understands domains as defined in DDD.

And now, we are at the core of the problem: DDD was not intended for data architecture, but for the creation of software. Thought leaders in the data mesh movement such as Zhamak Dehghani and Piethein Strengholt both point to DDD regarding how to organize data in domains.[3] And they both address that rescoping DDD for data and not software is far from easy and ideal—although they provide sound and applicable advice on how to do it. Nevertheless, for a data catalog in particular, I suggest taking another approach in understanding and designing domains, one that focuses less on software and more on knowledge. This approach is found in information science.

---

1 Eric Evans, *Domain-Driven Design: Tackling Complexity in the Heart of Software* (Upper Saddle River, NJ: Addison-Wesley, 2003).

2 Ibid., Part I.

3 Zhamak Dehghani, *Data Mesh: Delivering Data-Driven Value at Scale* (Sebastopol, CA: O'Reilly, 2021), 18; Strengholt talks about this problem as a guest on Data Mesh Radio (*https://oreil.ly/9Tf1x*), and he further discusses it in the article "Data Domains" (*https://oreil.ly/g4Whf*).

I'll first explain domain thinking in information science, and I'll then briefly discuss the differences between domain thinking in DDD and information science in a note.

In information science, a domain has no links to a technological reality per se. It's purpose is not to create software; it simply focuses on people and what they do, and it defines a domain like this:

> A domain, then, can be a group of people who work together if they share knowledge, goals, methods of operation, and communication. It can be a community of hobbyists, a scholarly discipline, an academic department, and so on.[4]

This is the definition of domain that I rely on in this book, and behind this very simple definition, it follows that a domain is made of:

- *Knowledge* as an ontological base,[5] meaning a shared understanding of concepts and their relations
- *Goals* as a teleology,[6] meaning that this group shares ambitions of what they want to achieve or obtain—what drives them
- *Methods* of operation, meaning hypotheses and methodologies to test and expand the domain
- *Communication* as social semantics, in the sense of what tools and systems the group uses to communicate

Each domain also has various degrees of *intension* and *extension*.[7]

The *intension* is how deep a domain goes in terms of the level of expert knowledge. For example, academics would have a deeper intension than hobbyists. Intension has a very concrete meaning: a domain can have an infinite layer of subdomains, so, for example, winemaking can have subdomains such as natural winemaking and traditional winemaking. In the case of the hobbyists, the intension stops there, but that would not be the case for the academics, who would further divide the intension of natural winemaking into organic winemaking and biodynamic winemaking and probably even further.

---

4 Richard P. Smiraglia, *The Elements of Knowledge Organization* (Cham: Springer, 2014), 86. The theoretical definition—cited from the same source—goes like this: "A domain is a group with an ontological base that reveals an underlying teleology, a set of common hypotheses, epistemological consensus on methodological approaches, and social semantics."

5 Ontology is the study of what exists—in this case, a domain.

6 Teleology is the study of what the intrinsic purpose inside something is—in this case, a domain.

7 Joseph T. Tennis, "Two Axes of Domains for Domain Analysis," *Knowledge Organization* 30, no. 3 (July 2003): 191–95.

Extension, on the other hand, refers to the level of breadth in the domain, and in this case, the hobbyists have a broader extension as they are likely to include adjacent domains into their own domain, without mastering them at a professional level. Winemaking would be part of a domain also comprising travel and pleasure, for example.

> The fundamental problem of applying DDD for data, in a data mesh, is that intension and extension are not free. Domains of various levels of intension and extension are put together in a string to define how data flows between software components. That may work for a data mesh orchestrated in an actual IT landscape, but it will not work in a data catalog: it will not deliver the total overview of data in your company in a structure that is searchable enough to create data discovery. To understand the difference, take a look at the domain mappings in Figure 2-3, and compare them with the data lineage depictions. If we were to accept only DDD for data as structuring our domains at the metadata level, then we would have to rely only on data lineage. This is technically correct but is conceptually confusing, as domains and subdomains are forced to structure themselves around the physical movement of data, and not the conceptual organization of data, thematically, in domains.

In Figure 2-3, I have added knowledge, goals, methods, and communication, as well as intension and extension, to our domain architecture diagram. These elements, which constitute a domain in information science, are all placed where they belong in the domain architecture of the data catalog. At this point, we are ready to run through the domain architecture in a data catalog, and I begin with the layer that can be structured based on either processes or capabilities.

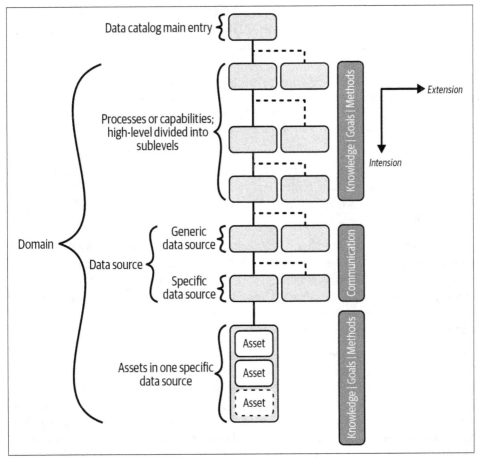

Figure 2-3. Domain architecture in a data catalog with domain-specific components

Processes and Capabilities

In this section, I am organizing data in a structure that represents the company in which the data is created. This structure is defined by either processes or capabilities.

Processes describe *how* a company performs its tasks. It's how things are done. Capabilities describe *what* tasks a company performs—what the company is capable of. Neither processes nor capabilities reflect the business units of your company 1:1.

Furthermore, processes are part of capabilities: capabilities consist of people, processes, and technology.

You can find a great introduction to processes and capabilities in *A Guide to the Business Architecture Body of Knowledge* (BIZBOK),[8] which I recommend you read before you actually begin mapping domains in your data catalog.

 I suggest you organize by capabilities if your data catalog is closely connected to the enterprise architecture activities, which rely on capability to manage the IT landscape. I suggest you use processes if your company already has a highly controlled process map.

The very first step to organizing your domain is to choose between creating the domains as processes or capabilities. Both will work fine, as they are stable entities. In either case, you start with high-level processes or capabilities and divide them into various sublevels.

A *process* domain is put together based on *how* things are done. Processes are part of a value chain that expresses *how* the products or services of a company are created. Processes are either directly or indirectly part of this value chain. Direct processes are, e.g., Research & Development, Manufacturing, and Sales. Indirect processes are supportive processes or strategic processes that enable the value chain, and they contain processes within themselves also.

In Figure 2-4 you can see an example of an indirect process map in the Hugin & Munin data catalog, namely HR processes. Pay attention to the process aspect in the level just below "HR Processes" that expresses how employees join, work in, and leave a company in the following process steps: Recruitment, Onboarding, Development, Self-Service, Offboarding, and Resignation. As you can see, all groupings are part of an overall process. Therefore, the domain depicted would partly lose its meaning if one of these parts were missing.

The knowledge, goals, and methods must be described in each part of the domain at the process level. Ideally, the processes displayed are self-explanatory, but you must ensure as logical an overview as possible for the end user of the data catalog.

---

8 See *A Guide to the Business Architecture Body of Knowledge* (Business Architecture Guild, version 11), specifically section 2.2 for capabilities and section 3.4 for processes.

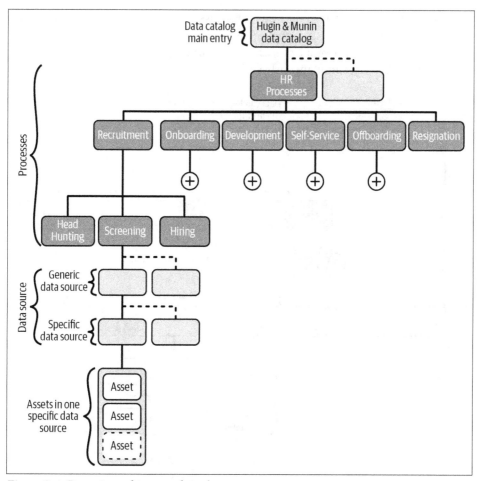

Figure 2-4. Domain architecture based on processes

A *capability* domain is put together based on *what* things are done. Capabilities are performed by many different business units and are therefore present in many different business processes. Unlike processes, capabilities are expressed using nouns, also for activities performed, typically coined as Management or Analytics, Determination, and Prioritization.

In Figure 2-5 you can see an example of a capability mapping in the data catalog, in this case, Data Analytics. I advise you to look closely at the level just below Data Analytics, containing the capabilities: Descriptive Analytics (what happened?), Diagnostic Analytics (why did it happen?), Predictive Analytics (what might happen?), and

Prescriptive Analytics (what should we do because of what will happen?).[9] Unlike the processes you saw in Figure 2-4, the capabilities are not part of a chain of events—they are not steps in an overall process. They can be performed by many different parts of your company, simultaneously and independently.

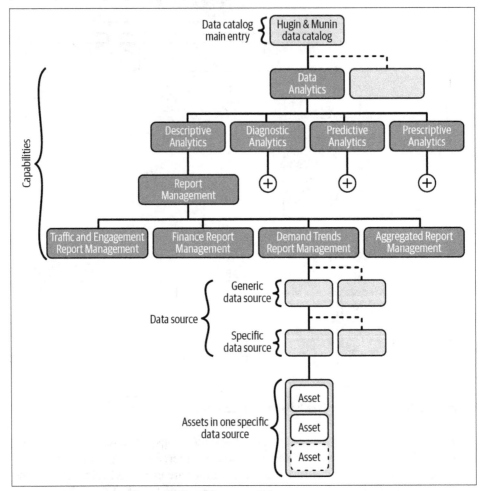

Figure 2-5. Domain architecture based on capabilities

Do not be tempted to build your domains directly based on your organization diagram. It's tempting to do so, because you have it at hand and mapped out for you already. But you must keep in mind that your domains should be stable entities to

---

9 A discussion of these capabilities can be found at "4 Types of Data Analytics Every Analyst Should Know—Descriptive, Diagnostic, Predictive, Prescriptive" (*https://oreil.ly/3FxiP*).

land data safely in the data catalog. And organizations change all the time: teams are merged, split up, outsourced, re-created, and reorganized constantly—and you end up maintaining a continuously changing domain architecture instead of catering to data discovery.

 If you work in a highly regulated industry, such as food, pharma, or oil and gas, your company has an official process map with several layers, contained in a quality management system (QMS).[10] It's a requirement for regulated industries to document their processes, as these industries must explain and show proof of correctly performed processes under audit and inspections from the authorities, such as the Food and Drug Administration (FDA) in the United States. If your company has such a process map, use it! You must organize your domains in the data catalog so that they mirror the process map 1:1, but you can leave out the lowest levels of the process map. They are typically too detailed and explain very specific actions by employees. Below the process levels, you should define data sources—take a look at Figure 2-4 if this puzzles you.

If your company does not have an existing process map, you can create either a process map or a capability map. You must remember not to mix processes and capabilities, as they are different in nature. You must choose one or the other and stick to that.

Now we move to the level below processes/capabilities, which is the technology layer—your actual data sources.

Data Sources

When you have successfully mapped your domain into processes or capabilities, you move deeper into the architecture and depict the data sources that support them. The generic data source is a technology component. These technologies can be databases, data lakes or data warehouses, and actual applications.

 Keep in mind that you cannot skip mapping domains in either processes or capabilities. Your map of data sources will be meaningless, close to unreadable for end users, if you move directly from the data catalog main entry and into generic data sources. Even the data discovery team will lose track of what data sources are registered in the data catalog if you proceed in such a way.

---

10 QMSs are specified in and must adhere to, e.g., ISO 9001:2015.

Let's continue with the Hugin & Munin capability domains example from the previous section. Take a look at Figure 2-6. Hugin & Munin uses Power BI as the data source to support the capability of *Demand Trends Report Management* (part of *Report Management*, part of *Descriptive Analytics*, part of *Data Analytics*). This is first registered as a generic data source, as there are many specific instances of Power BI, so you must remember to divide your data sources into generic and specific ones. The generic data source simply refers to the software component, such as Tableau, Qlik Sense, or, in this case, Power BI.

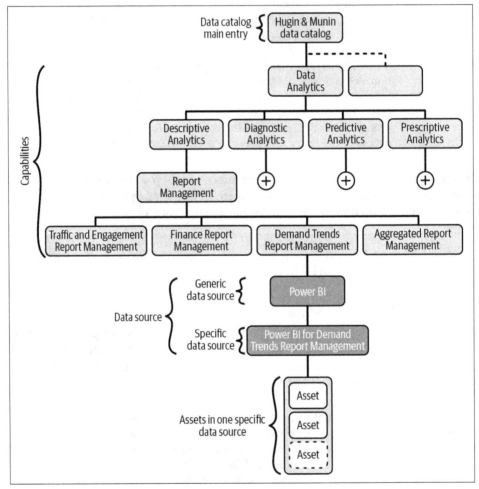

Figure 2-6. Generic and specific data source

You should not ignore creating the layers above the data sources, depicted in Figure 2-6. That comes with the risk of losing the capability to search for data, as the lack of organization makes it hard to understand where in the company the data comes from.

Below the generic data source is the specific data source. You need to treat each data source as a specific instance of a generic data source, so that the assets contained in the capability are the only ones supporting this capability. This will also ease how you assign roles and responsibilities to the assets.

A specific data source simply means that it is a specific instance of the generic data source. In this case, it's a specific subscription of Power BI. You must be aware that it could also be only part of a subscription; sometimes it's not relevant to expose all data.

Think of this from a domain perspective: your data sources are how the domain communicates. So how many data sources you have, and how much data from them you include in the domain, must be no more, no less, than the number of sources the domain uses to communicate.

The possibility to divide data sources like this is another advantage of an information scientific approach to domains. DDD domains always struggle with how to handle data sources (software) used in several domains, because they are rooted in software process thinking.

At this point, you have created a safe landing zone for data sources. Figure 2-2 to Figure 2-6 illustrated how you organize data: first in domains based on capabilities or processes, then in generic data sources, and finally in specific data sources, where you will place your collection of assets.

The first thing you need to do is to pull or push your assets from the data source into the data catalog.

Getting Assets into the Data Catalog

Getting assets into your data catalog by either pull or push is an enormous topic. You can read more about this in Chapter 6. But I must also advise you to consult other data management literature to get a complete picture of how push and pull is performed—for example, *Fundamentals of Data Engineering*.[11] If your company is in the process of selecting a data catalog, you can ask the sales engineers for specific guidance as well.

---

11 Joe Reis and Matt Housley, *Fundamentals of Data Engineering: Plan and Build Robust Data Systems* (Sebastopol, CA: O'Reilly, 2022).

For now, I will briefly introduce push and pull so that you get familiarized with the concepts and know what you need to prepare for when getting data into your data catalog. Let's begin with pull.

Pull

The *pull* principle is used by most data catalog providers. There are three scenarios for pull:

- Using standard connectors
- API
- Read-only data store (RDS) and built-in crawler

Pull is mostly done through *standard connectors*. These are built-in connectors, also called built-in crawlers, in the data catalog. The connector/crawler is a small program that is designed to run through a specific data source and export all metadata values in the source into the data catalog (see Figure 2-7). Each type of data source requires its own connector. Therefore, the types and numbers of connectors in a data catalog are something that you must consider carefully when you assess which one to buy. You can have a look in Chapter 6 in the section "Choosing a Data Catalog" regarding what you need to consider when selecting your data catalog.

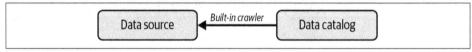

Figure 2-7. Using a standard connector (built-in crawler)

Nevertheless, you are likely to find yourself in a situation where you lack connectors to relevant data sources for your data catalog. The reason is that the number of IT systems is growing very fast these days; for example, take a look at the data and AI landscape (*https://oreil.ly/TVnB1*) just for technology focused on data. Remember that each application needs a distinct connector. No vendor is capable of producing connectors to all data sources out there.

In the case of unavailable connectors, you can use the *API* (see Figure 2-8).

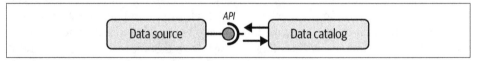

Figure 2-8. Using an API

What you need to know about APIs is this. You know that an application (an IT system) has a UI—that's the interface you use when you interact with the application. But sometimes, applications need to interact not with users, but with other applications. In that case, it is not the interface for users, the UI, that is relevant, but the interface for applications (application programming interface, API) that is relevant. Basically, using an API is like a phone call. API calls between applications send data from the data source into the consuming application.

But some data sources do not have an API layer, and therefore, you can resort to another relatively simple solution, depicted in Figure 2-9. This is to mirror your data source in an RDS. RDSs can be databases, data lakes, and other storage solutions: solutions where data is stored simply to be read (and not maintained or part of a business process orchestrated between several IT systems). The trick here is that you choose an RDS that can be crawled with an out-of-the-box connector in the data catalog.

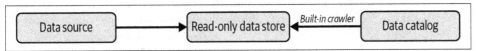

Figure 2-9. Using an RDS plus a standard connector (built-in crawler)

Push

Push is typically based on streaming. Very simply explained, with streaming you don't make "phone calls." You just sit and listen. Streaming literally illustrates that you do not influence what data you receive, the stream does. When you stream on, e.g., Netflix, you sit and listen to the stream, you do not call a data source via an API. Streaming is a technology that filters data from source systems into channels on a (streaming) platform. On that platform, consumers—such as a data catalog—can choose to subscribe to channels with various data. (Technically speaking, you connect to a streaming platform using an API layer. The push happens between the data source and the streaming platform.)

Streaming—push—as the sole ingestion method in a data catalog is rare. The data catalog Acryl that is built on DataHub uses it. But push is time-consuming and requires data quality to be high up front. You can see a conceptual overview of the basic push scenario in Figure 2-10.

Figure 2-10. Basic push scenario

The pros and cons of streaming/pushing data in data catalogs are that it is useful if you are in need of a real-time data catalog, with ultrafresh, updated data. However, streaming is costly, and you may consider if it is necessary. I discuss this in greater detail in Chapter 6.

The pros and cons of crawling/pulling data are that it gives you a cheaper, easier, but not-as-updated data catalog. But in most cases, a data catalog will work fine in this setup, unless you really need live data.

Let's sum up. You now know how to structure a domain inside your data catalog and how to pull or push data into that domain. Here, the data will appear as assets representing data in a data source. Next, you need to organize your assets in your domain and understand what kind of metadata you need to add to assets and why.

Organizing Assets in the Domains

How well you organize your assets inside their domain will determine if your data catalog is a success or a failure. Assets that are not assigned relevant metadata will slowly disappear in the total number of assets—they will not appear in searches by the end users of the data catalog. You need your assets to be discovered and used, and this section will teach you how.

Asset Metadata

I defined *asset* in Chapter 1 as an entity of data that exists in your IT landscape. It could be a file, folder, or table, stored in a data source such as an application or database, etc. The asset in the data catalog consists of metadata that represents that file, folder, schema, and so on in the data source. *Metadata* is popularly defined as "data about data." This definition is short but precise. To elaborate, metadata *refers* to other data, and it does not exist without the data it refers to. Assets are made up entirely of metadata; all your assets in your data catalog *refer* to data in data sources. In the sections that follow, you will learn to describe your assets so that you maximize their data discovery potential.

All assets have owners and stewards. Consider these roles as mandatory metadata: all assets need to have assigned owners and stewards. *Asset owners* are the actual owners of data in the source system. It will always be the data owner who defines who can access a data source and what data can be used for.

It's a strategic gain for your company that the data catalog can help assign data ownership. This is a very difficult task in most companies, due to the common lack of understanding of this responsibility—it's complex and only offers hardship. With a data catalog, that's different: data ownership suddenly comes with services such as an overview of sensitive data and a control mechanism of *how* data owners share data.

In daily operations, it will be the *asset steward* who maintains assets in a domain. Specifically, the asset steward adds metadata and handles data access requests and lifecycle management activities in general—check out Chapter 7 about lifecycles.

To properly organize the assets in a domain, you need to think about how the metadata for each asset was derived or added to the data catalog. The metadata for an asset can be derived from a data source, it can be added when the asset is already in the data catalog, or both.

On a more general level, assets can have:

- Metadata derived from the data source
- Metadata added in the data catalog
- Metadata *either* derived from the data source *or* added in the data catalog

Let's go through each scenario.

Metadata derived from the data source

There are two types of metadata in an asset that are always derived from the data source:

- Technical metadata
- Business metadata

Technical metadata tells you exactly what data source the asset is stored in, who created the asset, when the asset was created, the file format of the asset, etc. Its data is automatically attached to an asset, during its creation and existence. For example, a Qlik Sense report created by a business analyst in the HR department on December 13, 2021, based on JavaScript and QEXT files.

Business metadata is metadata that describes the asset in human language, for example names of tables and columns, descriptions and definitions of data types, etc.

Derived metadata constitutes the minimum description of your assets. It's valuable, and you need it to get the facts right about your assets, but you can't rely on derived metadata alone: it will not contextualize your assets sufficiently to make your data catalog perform relevant search experiences for end users—people won't find what they are looking for. Therefore, you need to add metadata to your assets inside the data catalog.

Metadata added in the data catalog

You can add metadata such as descriptions, people, and glossary terms to the assets in your data catalog. You can also modify the metamodel of the data catalog to better make it express the logic of your company (I discuss classifications separately, later).

Descriptions are high-level descriptions of assets, and they should contain at least two elements: primary and secondary usage. *Primary usage* is a brief explanation about what the asset is used for in the data source where it was pulled/pushed from.

Secondary usage is suggestions from the data provider to potential consumers about what the asset can be used for.

People are all the relevant persons who should be listed in the data catalog. These are, for example:

- Domain owner
- Domain steward
- Data source owner
- Asset owner
- Asset steward
- Term owner
- Term steward

The *domain owner* is the owner of a given domain and is responsible for managing the domain. Typically, this person will also be who data management usually thinks of as a *data owner*, as this role spans several data sources. The *domain steward* is responsible for curating a domain and providing access to sources. The *data source owner* is the owner of a given IT system. The *asset owner* is the person who has created the asset. The *asset steward* is typically responsible for managing the practical work of managing many assets. The *term owner* owns a domain term or a global term. Free glossary terms do not have ownership, as they are unmanaged. The *term steward* manages several terms.

Glossary terms are basically words that are found in various glossaries inside the data catalog. Glossaries allow you to "tag" your asset with terms. This increases the discoverability of the asset when users search for topics where the asset could be relevant. The glossaries are lists of words that describe your company, and the glossaries are controlled to various degrees, by either a domain glossary team or a centralized global glossary team.

Figure 2-11 illustrates three different glossary types:

- Free glossary
- Domain glossary
- Global glossary

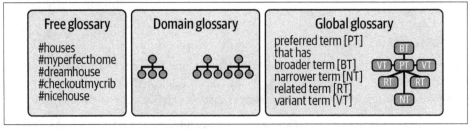

Figure 2-11. Glossary types

The *free glossary* is a folksonomy (*https://oreil.ly/eJfOp*). Folksonomies are user-generated glossaries that organize assets by the use of tags. If you use social media, you've probably seen posts relating to a certain topic marked with a hashtag. For example, #puppies for posts involving dogs, #ootd for posts about someone's outfit of the day, or more seriously, #metoo for posts about sexual harassment. There are no formal rules in a folksonomy; everyone can create tags and use them as they want. However, don't let its use on social media fool you into thinking they're just for fun. In a data catalog, you can use a folksonomy to describe assets in completely unique ways, and this will enable you to search for specific topics that a central team would not have thought of.

A *domain glossary* is a taxonomy. Taxonomies have a hierarchy. They can be narrow/broad or have facets of narrow/broad relationships of terms. It is a user-generated glossary that organizes assets by the use of terms that are agreed upon and aligned on the domain level. Taxonomies are more controlled than folksonomies. Taxonomies are created by a small group of people within a domain and not the general public—or the entire group of employees in a company—and, subsequently, the taxonomy creates a more formal language. Tags are completely free associations; for example, *#ootd* in the folksonomy might be *daily clothes* in a taxonomy. This is because a group within a domain has decided a logical term to describe this specific element of clothing. Also, taxonomies tend to create hierarchies between terms, some being broader than others; for example, *daily clothes* is a narrower term than *clothes* but broader than *daily clothes when it rains*. Some taxonomies, especially in online shopping experiences, apply a faceted approach that enables the user to "build" a unique expression when organizing data and searching. Such facets could be colors: e.g., *blue* + garment, e.g., *dress*. This is certainly also applicable in data catalogs, and as you will see in Chapter 3, a faceted approach can be of great benefit. Taxonomies are domain specific. They represent a domain's formal description of itself in a glossary. The taxonomy alternative to the folksonomy is also very useful when searching the data catalog, as you will see in Chapters 3 and 4.

The *global glossary* is a *thesaurus* (*https://oreil.ly/Wjpeo*). It's a structure that moves away from hierarchy thinking and toward cluster thinking instead. It has a center, the preferred term (PT). This is the core of the cluster, the main thing that is described. Let's stick to the above example and say that the preferred term is *daily clothes*. This preferred term is surrounded by variant terms (VTs), which are synonyms. In this case, a VT could be *#ootd*. There are also more freely associated terms, called related terms (RTs). In this case, it could be, for example, *raincoat*. Finally, there are narrower terms (NTs), for example, *daily clothes when it rains*, and broader terms (BTs), in this case *clothes*. But keep in mind that it is the PT that is the center of the cluster; it may have as many BTs as you see fit, and it does not belong in an overall hierarchy. An ontology is highly controlled and has a lot of potential for improving search, as you'll see in Chapter 3.

From a systemic point of view, you lose the ability to analyze and improve search behavior if you believe you have perfectly described the truth of your company in a highly controlled glossary. You must strive for both no control and control at the same time.

 Do not assume that more-controlled glossaries are less biased than glossaries where you have little or no control over the terms. What you get with control is a more consistent semantic expression, globally in your glossary, between your terms. But it will be just as subjective and biased a glossary as a loosely controlled glossary. For example, Melissa Adler has succinctly examined the gender and race bias in the cataloging practice in the Library of Congress in the United States.[12]

Do not take the implementation and management of your glossaries lightly. They are the cornerstone in improving your data catalog's search capability. You'll learn the organizational details in the rest of this chapter, and you'll realize how in Chapter 3.

 A glossary is not to be confused with a *data dictionary*. The data dictionary is a basic tool that specifies the types of data you have at a generic level, typically by listing the field name and providing a description of the kind of data the field contains. The data dictionary is a natural part of data catalogs and may not always be a separate feature, but simply included directly in the assets. A glossary, on the other hand, is an interpretation and reflection of the data that contextualizes this data into the overall knowledge of your company.

Finally, you can change the *metamodel*. In Chapter 1, I mentioned that data catalogs sometimes have flexible metamodels. Metamodel flexibility can be provided at various levels. The most advanced and useful level of metamodel flexibility is provided in knowledge graph–based data catalogs. The metamodels of such data catalogs have these characteristics:[13]

The metamodel is visual.
    It's a browsable metamodel that you can see—a structure that shows how all entities are connected.

---

12 Melissa Adler, *Cruising the Library: Perversities in the Organization of Knowledge* (New York: Fordham University Press, 2017).

13 Juan Sequeda, "What Does It Mean for a Data Catalog to Be Powered by a Knowledge Graph?" (*https://oreil.ly/c6l0p*), September 2022, Datanami.com.

The metamodel is extendable.
    You can add new entities to your metamodel and likewise create new relations.

The metamodel is searchable.
    This means, basically, that you can query everything in the data catalog using a database query language like SPARQL.

In the context of this section, you should consider that the metamodel is extendable. This means that you can add entities to the metamodel. For example, in the case of Hugin & Munin, the metamodel could be extended with entities that represent data from the people and systems that treat wood, from the moment it is cut, to how it is inventoried as lumber, to the final building in which it is used.

Adding a specific business context is useful for the metamodel, because you can now link all the data that is associated to this business context. This will improve your ability to organize data and search for it.

You can also get metadata just by crawling, as described in the next section.

Metadata derived from the data source or added in the data catalog

Certain types of metadata are included as derived metadata.

Data lineage and semantic relations as graphs are important metadata to each asset. I defined both of them in Chapter 1, but let me briefly recap. *Data lineage* shows how an entire asset travels horizontally, in an ETL/ELT (extract, transform, load/extract, load, transform) process. *Semantic relations* show parts of an asset (e.g., a specific column in a table) and how it relates to parts of other assets.

Both lineage and semantic relations are technical features. At a bare minimum, lineage visualizes ETL jobs in certain data sources, and semantic relations are built on a graph database that can be combined with natural language processing and machine learning in cases where it is derived from the data source. You should be able to expand both, manually and via API, inside the data catalog.

Figure 2-12 shows the asset architecture of Hugin & Munin. Notice that it builds on Figures 1-3 and 2-3, which showed a fully organized asset and a domain architecture built on capabilities. What you see is a generic Power BI asset, including all the metadata types I have discussed in this section. The straight lines from the central asset and outward are lineage, and they depict the lineage of the entire dataset, where it comes from and where it travels further. The curved lines from the central asset and outward are graph relations, and they depict parts of the asset being conceptually/semantically related to other assets.

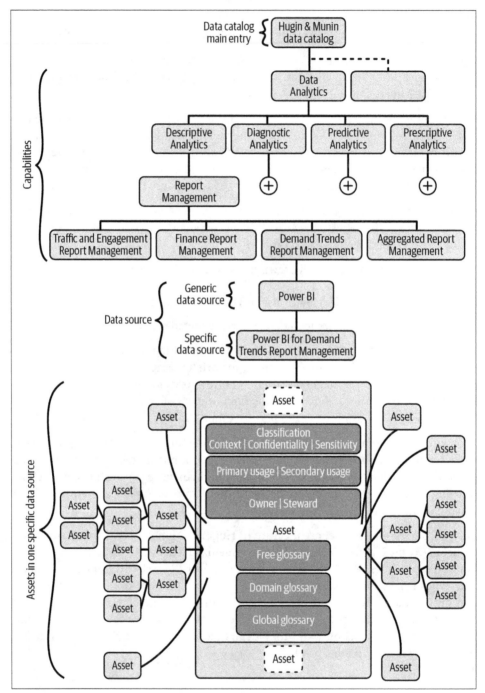

Figure 2-12. Asset architecture

Metadata Quality

In this section, I discuss how to analyze the quality of domains and assets in the data catalog. Because everything in the data catalog consists of metadata, I call this analysis *metadata quality.*[14] Metadata quality refers to how well domains and their assets are represented. Without metadata of descriptions, people, and glossary terms, the search functions in your data catalog will not work well.

> Your ability to search a data catalog depends on the quality of this metadata—not on the quality of the data in your data sources!

Earlier in this chapter, I discussed intension (depth) and extension (width) of domains. These two things constitute the *actual* depth and width of the domain—how the domain happens to be architected in your data catalog.

But there are also *ideal* depths and widths of domains. They are not universal (no universal, ideal domain architecture exists). The ideal depth and width of a domain is based on a domain analysis and is expressed with one term, for both depth and width: exhaustivity.

> Domain analysis is an essential part of information science. If you need to perform a domain analysis, take an initial look at Smiraglia's book, which I quoted earlier in this chapter. It contains a list of the methods usually applied.

Exhaustivity characterizes a state where a domain is perfectly expressed in depth and width. Exhaustivity, therefore, can be high if the domain is depicted in perfect depth and width. Likewise, exhaustivity is low if the domain is depicted in insufficient depth and width. This goes for its structure in the overall domain map, and it goes for all its associated metadata.

Let's say, for example, that the only global glossary term for the building material in Hugin & Munin is Wood. This is an unacceptable, low level of exhaustivity. All the buildings that Hugin & Munin design are made of wood, so the glossary would need to go into depth about what kind of wood was used for which buildings. Was it beech or pine for the family house just outside Oslo? Was it oak for the skyscraper in

---

14 I do not discuss how you analyze the data quality of the data sources that the data catalog depicts—it's another discipline that you can find numerous sources on. In most of those standards, data quality and metadata quality are interwoven and made measurable, e.g., FAIR (*https://oreil.ly/Z5XY2*) (findable, accessible, interoperable, and reusable).

downtown Stockholm? The exhaustivity of the glossary needs to align with the domain in scope. If the exhaustivity is too low, then the glossary can't be used, functionally, to depict the domain, and then searching for data won't work. But even if the level of exhaustivity is perfect, things can go wrong. You need to get familiarized with specificity also.

Specificity is the *usage* of the *actual* intension (depth) and extension (width) in the domain—and not a potential usage of the exhaustivity. So if you, e.g., have only pulled or pushed data sources to a few of the actual subdomains in your domain, then exhaustivity is high and the specificity is low. Likewise, if you have pulled or pushed data sources to most subdomains in your domain, then your specificity is high.

Let's return to the example above: Wood. Say that the global glossary contains the words Beech, Oak, Pine, and Wood—and that this level of exhaustivity is acceptably high for Hugin & Munin. Now, what happens if the only glossary term that assets have been tagged with is Wood? Then, exhaustivity is high, but specificity is low. This means, basically, that your search features could have worked because the assets could have been tagged with the most appropriate terms from the glossary (the exhaustivity is high), but that search does not work because those glossary terms were not applied.

If the glossary terms for a specific domain cover the domain appropriately, then the level of exhaustivity is high. If they do not, then the level of exhaustivity is low. This is the case if the glossary terms are too broad or simply lacking. If all or most of the glossary terms for a specific domain are applied to some of the assets in the domain, then the specificity is high. If they are not, specificity is low.

Figure 2-13 provides an overview of how to think about exhaustivity and specificity. It's a matrix, because you basically have four scenarios for exhaustivity/specificity, either both are low or high, or one is high and one is low. We'll return to this specificity/exhaustivity matrix in Chapters 3 and 4.

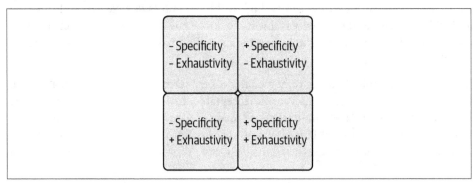

Figure 2-13. Specificity/exhaustivity matrix for metadata

Exhaustivity and specificity are important for search. We'll talk about it more in Chapter 3, but here are some questions for you to think about in the meantime: Is it easy to search for a very special type of asset, if it has been cataloged with only general, broad glossary terms although more specific terms exist in the glossary? Is it easy to browse your way to a very special type of asset in a domain, if the domain only has few, very broad subdomains? Can you trust that you have searched correctly, if the only hits you get on something very general are detailed, specialized assets?

Classification

The metadata of a data catalog may include metadata from the data sources themselves, as well as glossary terms added in the data catalog, but it also includes the classification of assets. So, what does it mean to classify something?

Classification can mean several things, depending on whom you ask. For example, you might hear the following dialogue between a CISO and a DPO:

CISO: "I have classified this data … and it is highly confidential!"

DPO: "What do you mean? I classified this data months ago; it's not sensitive at all."

CISO: "What? I completely disagree!"

DPO: "Huh? So do I!"

In fact, both the CISO and the DPO have correctly classified the data—it's often the case that data is classified as highly confidential and not sensitive at all, at the same time. This is exactly because classification can mean different things. There are three types of classification:

- Content
- Confidentiality
- Sensitivity

In your data catalog, you must enable all three types of classifications on each asset, and users must be able to combine them as they want. Remember: high levels of confidentiality do not imply high levels of sensitivity, and vice versa.

Classification of content refers to what your asset is. It's the unique label of your asset that defines exactly what it is about. I advise you to build the content classification in the data catalog based on the structure of your domains—and that you formalize this in instructions to domain owners, so that the content classification is consistently applied. For example, the following expresses the classification of content for an asset in the Hugin & Munin data catalog shown in Figure 2-6:

DA.DeA.RM.DT.Power BI

The logic of this expression is that all the capabilities as acronyms are shortened so they are all distinguishable from each other, combined with the generic data source. You can see the expression visually explained in Figure 2-14.

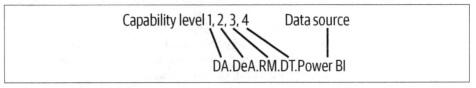

Figure 2-14. Methodology for content classification

So, this asset is within the Data Analytics (DA) domain, under Descriptive Analytics (DeA), under Report Management (RM), within Demand Trends (DT), and uses Power BI as the data source. As you will learn in Chapter 3, content classification is a very powerful element to search your data catalog. You may find it cumbersome to define content classification for each specific subdomain of assets and make users apply it, but these processes can be automated in data catalogs. And the payoff really is remarkable.

Classification of confidentiality is how secret your asset is. All your assets have a level of confidentiality. Your CISO is the defining authority of confidentiality, in close collaboration with the legal counsel. Confidentiality classifications originate from military, police, and intelligence organizations. The North Atlantic Treaty Organization (NATO (*https://oreil.ly/oiRWl*)) has the following confidentiality classifications:

- COSMIC TOP SECRET
- NATO SECRET
- NATO CONFIDENTIAL
- NATO RESTRICTED

Also, the label UNCLASSIFIED is added to open, public information in NATO. The level of confidentiality is determined by the level of damage a breach of the data would cause. The exposure of COSMIC TOP SECRET data from inside NATO will cause *exceptionally grave damage*, NATO SECRET will cause *serious damage*, NATO CONFIDENTIAL will cause *damage to the interests of NATO*, and finally NATO RESTRICTED will *be disadvantageous to NATO*.

Although it's generally good practice to err on the side of caution, the extreme can be detrimental.[15] If all data in your data catalog is TOP SECRET, then you end up with a cumbersome security structure, and you lose the point of the data catalog: to make data discoverable, and therefore used in new contexts. You need to be realistic about how confidential your data actually is. Think about it this way: if the data were to be accidentally released, how much damage would it cause? A document containing an SOP for cleaning a production facility is relatively harmless. A BI report containing the production performance of the production facility would be less harmless, but not life-threatening to the company. A drawing in DWG format of the production facility in complete detail would be catastrophic in terms of industrial espionage, if it were accidentally made public.

Classification of sensitivity is how personal your asset is.[16] All your assets have a level of sensitivity. It is the DPO who ensures that the various regulations on personal identifiable information (PII) are enforced in your company—as such, it is considered a core part of data governance. If your company is operating on a global scale, these are the levels of sensitivity you must choose between and assign to your assets in the data catalog:

- Nonpersonal data
- PII
  — Personal data
  — Sensitive personal data

PII is a global term that merely distinguishes between data that is not personal and data that is. Personal data simply means that the data in question can identify a person. In the General Data Protection Regulation (GDPR), PII is further distinguished between personal data and sensitive personal data. Personal data is private, but not compromising; for example, name, address, and age. Personal sensitive data, on the other hand, is compromising data, and includes, for example, membership of a union, political party, ethnicity, and health data. Many data catalogs can automatically detect if an asset holds a value that is PII, so this classification can be automated.

---

15 The most tragic example of that is the terror attacks in the United States on September 11, 2001. The Congressional Research Service concluded in 2011 (*https://oreil.ly/10PTO*) that the terror attacks could likely have been avoided if a less restrictive confidentiality classification had been applied in various ways between the CIA and the FBI.

16 The reality is that the personal information can be difficult to ascertain, as several nonpersonal data together constitute personal information. See Sille Obelitz Søe et al., "What Is the 'Personal' in 'Personal Information'?" *Ethics and Information Technology* 23 (2021): 625–33.

Your data catalog has a big selling point. Normally, your CISO and DPO will oppose solutions that let all employees see all data in the company. But as data catalogs contain only metadata, not only will the CISO and DPO be OK with this solution, they will support it, because they get something they didn't have before. The CISO can control confidentiality, and the DPO can control sensitivity on the actual IT landscape and not just in policies.

Summary

In this chapter we discussed how to organize data in a data catalog. Here are the key takeaways of the chapter:

- Data sources in your data catalog are organized into domains. The information scientific understanding of domains is the one used in this book, as it is less software-centric and more conceptual than the one in domain-driven design.

- The domain structure has three layers that consist of processes or capabilities, data sources, and assets.

- Each layer has metadata.

- At the asset layer, there are three types of glossaries, namely folksonomies, taxonomies, and ontologies, and they all play an important role in describing your assets.

- Data sources are pulled and pushed into a data catalog, using out-of-the-box crawlers from the data catalog, read-only data stores (RDSs), APIs, and streaming.

- Classification means several things, namely classification of content, confidentiality, and sensitivity. All three are combined freely, because all kinds of data can be, e.g., highly confidential and not sensitive at all.

- The data catalog format is a structure that in itself summarizes the content of this chapter, as it structures all metadata that is necessary to assign to an asset in a data catalog.

In the next chapter, we will talk about how you search for data in a data catalog.

CHAPTER 3

Understand Search: Concepts, Features, and Mechanics

You now know how to organize data in your data catalog: you create your domains, pull or push your data sources into them, and add metadata. Now, you're ready to search your data catalog.

But why should you search a data catalog? What is it, exactly, you are searching for in a data catalog? And how do you actually search? How good is your simple search? How can you browse through data? And how can you search complex topics? These are the questions I discuss in this chapter.

In this chapter, we will discuss why, what, and how you search a data catalog. We will also cover the mechanics of search in order to deepen your understanding of how a data catalog functions.

First off, let's discuss the *why*.

Why Do You Search in a Data Catalog?

Why do you search a data catalog? The short answer is actually "for data discovery."

If you ask an average employee, "Why do you search a data catalog?" they might say, "Because I need information to solve a problem." If you ask governance end users, they might say, "Because we need to know what info we have to ensure that we are compliant with laws." If you ask a data analytics end user, they might say, "Because we want data to analyze trends and make improvements."

All three answers are correct, and all three answers have to do with data discovery. If you want to know what kind of data you have in your organization, the data catalog is the place to search. It's where your data discovery begins.

In Chapter 1 we discussed three types of end users in data catalogs:

- Everyday end users
- Governance end users
- Data analytics end users

Each of these end users should use the data catalog as their point of departure for any search process. Let's go through the end users one by one.

Everyday end users are all employees in your company—including yourself. Think of end users as a group of people who are just as diverse as all the employees of your company. In Hugin & Munin, everyday end users span architects, engineers, sales reps, a variety of craftspeople, and many more.

End users are looking for all kinds of stuff—say, a document or an SOP or analytical insight about our own business area. Everyday end users have information needs that arise from doing their job properly. Users will typically search in fast, simple ways, just typing one or two words and hoping to find the one right hit.

As data catalogs are evolving into company search engines, everyday end users will emerge, but they are not yet a widespread user group in most data catalogs. You will see more everyday user scenarios and how they will evolve in the future in Chapter 8.

Governance end users are those who are in charge of your company's data governance program. This includes, for example, compliance managers and staff of your DPO or CISO. For these types of end users, the data catalog offers true data discovery: an automated, powerful alternative to the often manually updated lists of data that these employees have had up until this point. The data catalog will give data governance end users a fresh, up-to-date overview of the data that is actually in the organization. With this overview provided by the data catalog, governance end users can improve the management of personal identifiable data and confidential data, and they can work on improving data quality and increase the retrieval speed of data in critical situations.

Data analytics end users are very familiar with data discovery; they are data scientists or perhaps data engineers. To them, data discovery means something very specific. They are used to searching in large datasets for patterns that provide analytical insights. But they often have a big problem: what is the best data to perform their analysis on? Often, these employees work not with the best data, but with the data they know. Data catalogs can help solve this problem by giving these end users a way to search for the best data to perform their analysis. To this type of end user, the data catalog is a little bit of a magic wand: it's a structured overview of all the data you can perform analysis on. It makes the data that is selected for subsequent analysis more fit and with a higher potential of success. Indeed, this type of end user is the very reason data catalogs are gaining such importance in many organizations today.

There is also a fourth type of end user. However, this end user is both to be found within the three mentioned categories and as a separate type: it's the *data engineer*. The data engineer is moving data from providers of data to consumers of data, and in that process, it is important to know the data sources. That is done with the data catalog.

Before we dive into the what and how of searching in data catalogs, here is an overview of ways to search.

Search Features in a Data Catalog

Basically, you can search a data catalog by simple search, browse, glossary, and advanced search. All vendors will have these features, but they look slightly different in all data catalogs. Figure 3-1 shows the Hugin & Munin data catalog's search features. By typing directly in the search bar, you perform a simple search; by clicking the Advanced button, you get the option to do an advanced search; click the magnifying glass and you can browse; and finally, if you click the pile of books icon, you search only the glossaries.

 Remember that this is the UI of the data catalog in Hugin & Munin. Your data catalog's UI will look a little different, but the search features will be there.

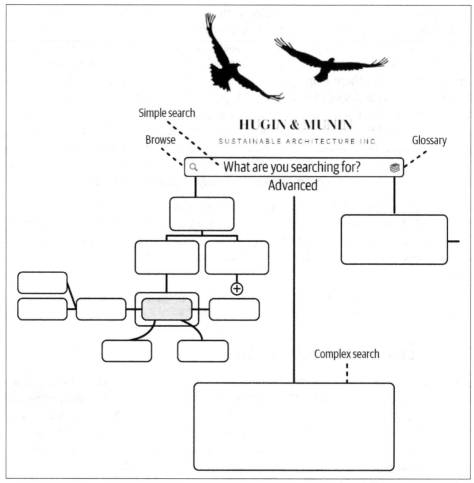

Figure 3-1. Typical search features in a data catalog

I will run through these in a moment, but first you need to get familiarized with an important distinction.

Searching in Data Versus Searching for Data

What do you search in a data catalog? One of the key things that you need to understand when working with a data catalog is that, when you search a data catalog, you are searching for data, not in data. There's a clear distinction between the two that will drive how you interact with the data catalog.

So, what's the difference between searching in data versus for data?

Searching *in* data is when we search in the actual data for something we want to know. For example, we might ask: "How many people looked at our website last Saturday night?" The answer to this is a value from access records: 1,000 people looked at our website last Saturday night.

Searching *for* data is when we search for the sources that contain the data we need. For example, we might ask: "Where can we find data about traffic on our website?" The answer will be a data location. We are not searching in the actual data, we are searching for the sources that hold the data.

As you can see, searching in data and searching for data go hand in hand. Once we find the data we are searching *for*, we can search *in* that data.

Searching *in* data is done with a *database query language* (DQL), illustrated in Figure 3-2. A DQL enables you to write statements and query different database technologies in the database's database management system (DBMS). The possibilities are endless; you can combine as many types of data in as complex ways as you want, since the DQLs are capable of performing intricate mathematical query statements on the data you're searching in. Quite logically, data science has emerged from this. Data scientists search directly in data, using DQLs at an advanced level. Data science looks for patterns, connections, and correlations in (very) large amounts of data.

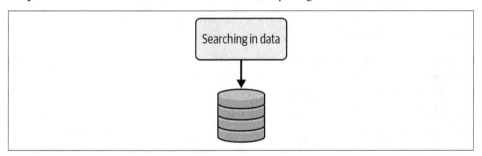

Figure 3-2. Searching in data

The most popular DQL is Structured Query Language (SQL). It allows you to perform queries by writing SQL statements in a DBMS to a relational database. Basically, you can "ask" anything if you master SQL well enough and your relational database holds the relevant kind of data. So, for example, you could ask about customer behavior at certain hours of the day, across a large geographical area, divided into many specific locations. To do this, you would translate what you want to know into an SQL statement, run it in the DBMS, and analyze the results. Further, the results you would get could be turned into business intelligence (BI) dashboards with reports, telling you and business leaders about interesting details on consumer behavior at certain hours of the day across a large geographical area.

In computer science and the data community in general, it is well-known what languages you can use when you search in data, but there is far less attention on the languages you use when you search for data.

Although there's a ton of literature out there for how to use DQLs to search in data, there's actually not much out there in data management literature about how to search for data. The *Data Management Body of Knowledge* (DAMA-DMBOK) mentions that: "Metadata repositories must have a front-end application that supports the search-and-retrieval functionality required."[1]

And that's it. That's the one(!) sentence on searching *for* data, in a data catalog,[2] in the entire DAMA-DMBOK, the go-to literature for data management. No search functionality is discussed, no techniques are displayed.

Instead of relying on only data management literature, we can broaden our horizons and consider guidance from another area of study—library and information science (LIS). LIS has thoroughly studied searching for data for ages.[3]

In LIS, you will find that there is a parallel dimension of query languages, next to DQL. It's a dimension of query languages that is completely missing in data management literature, as these languages have not been created by data managers and scientists. These languages are known as information retrieval query languages (IRQLs). IRQL has been developed by librarians, archivists, records managers, and most importantly: not data scientists, but information scientists.

But what's the role of an IRQL? IRQL allows all kinds of searches, from very simple to very complex searches. But that sounds just like DQLs, right? You're correct: IRQL does the same thing as DQL. The difference lies in what data layer the languages are applied on: you use DQLs to search *in* data, and you use IRQLs to search *for* data.

To match DQL and IRQL with databases, LIS operates with two kinds of databases:

- Source databases that hold data
- Reference databases that hold metadata about data stored elsewhere

---

1 Mark Mosley et al. (eds.), *DAMA-DMBOK: Data Management Body of Knowledge* (Vancouver, WA: DAMA International, 2010), 440.

2 Data catalogs are discussed together with other tools grouped as "metadata" repositories.

3 The most complete overview of studies in search is found in Jutta Haider and Olof Sundin, *Invisible Search and Online Search Engines: The Ubiquity of Search in Everyday Life* (London: Routledge, 2019); see especially chap. 2: "Perspectives on Search."

Chowdhury writes that the fundamental difference between the two kinds of databases are that: "Reference databases lead the users to the source of information. ... Source databases provide the answer with no need for the user to refer elsewhere."[4]

A reference database is a concept, not a specific technology. In Figure 3-3, a reference database holding metadata is illustrated at the left. Once you have searched *for* data and found it, in a data catalog, you are referred to the database in question, and you can continue your search activities there, searching *in* data.

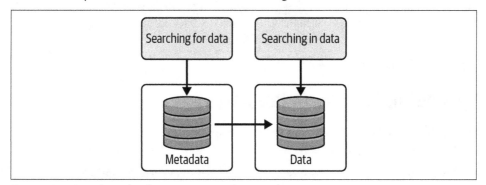

Figure 3-3. Searching for data versus searching in data

Traditionally, information science deals with three kinds of reference databases, namely:

Bibliographic databases
Lists of books on a given topic

Catalog databases
The collection of books of one or more libraries

Referral databases
Persons, companies, technologies, etc. on a given topic

I would add a fourth reference database to this list:

The data catalog
The collection of data in a given company

So there you have it. The data catalog is a reference database. To search it, you can't use DQL, because you are not searching *in* data. Instead, you can use IRQL, the query languages in scope for reference databases that allow you to search *for* and locate the data so you can use it.

---

4 G. G. Chowdhury, *Introduction to Modern Information Retrieval* (New York: Neal-Schuman Publishers, 2010), 17.

Furthermore, searching for data and searching in data can be defined as a spectrum of search, as seen in Figure 3-4. This spectrum goes from very simple searches to search procedures that are very difficult to conduct.

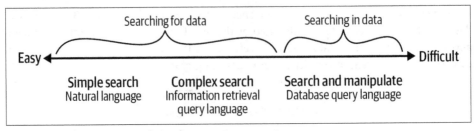

Figure 3-4. The spectrum of search

How Do You Search a Data Catalog?

Now that you know what you can search for in a data catalog and why, it's time to discuss how to actually do the search.

In this section, we will discuss query languages for data catalogs and the search features in a data catalog.

Data Catalog Query Language

Although searching a data catalog can be as simple as typing something into a search box and getting results, it's so much more than that. Today, searching a data catalog involves a combination of query language commands, operators, and clickable filters. Although this is not a complete, distinct query that end users can write and execute independently, it is the method or language in which we can communicate our needs to a data catalog.

> For the examples in this book, I've created a data catalog query language (DCQL) that is based on IRQLs and is representative of many real-life DCQLs today. Compare the DCQL search commands and operators in the Appendix to your own data catalog's DCQL and you will discover that they will be very similar. All data catalogs already use parts of DCQL-like language, so it should feel familiar to you.

With DCQL, as in any query language, you must pay close attention to syntax and semantics. When using DCQL, you are not helped by features behind the scenes as when using simple search and browsing; everything relies on you mastering your search via correct syntax and semantics.

Syntax is the specific meaning of an element in your search. When you search, you need to know the exact way to express a value. Be it the spelling of a glossary term, the precise format of, e.g., the serial numbers of your company product, or whatever, you have to apply correct syntax; if not, your search simply won't work.

Semantics is the overall meaning of your query statement. Does what you have written actually search for what you want to find? Are you lacking elements—could some be left out or do they negatively impact the search? Have you mixed up the logic of your search somehow with your operators? If you do not have correct semantics, your search will still run, but the result will be wrong. Your search hits won't be what you are actually looking for.

Keep in mind also that search can only be performed on what is in the data catalog. If data sources are poorly tagged with glossary terms, have no people associated with them, and so on, then the searches performed may be of good quality but will not provide useful search hits. How you organize data defines how you can search it.

I suggest you glance at the DCQL tables in the Appendix—not read them in the first go. Instead, read the following sections, look at the way search is performed, and go back to the DCQL tables and find the explanations of the details in the search examples.

The Search Features in a Data Catalog Explained

In this section, we will go through simple search, browse, glossary, and advanced search. Let's look at them one at a time, starting with the one that is the easiest to use.

Simple search

The first thing you need to know about simple search is that it really is simple: all you need to do is type a word or two in the search bar in order to get results. For example, you can search for "data analytics" in the Hugin & Munin data catalog, shown in Figure 3-5, and then you can expect to get a list of good hits with the most precise one on top. Just like that—simple!

The second thing you need to know about simple search is that it is not simple. The reason why it is not simple is because the algorithm performing the search is doing calculations behind the scenes. In Figure 3-5, the data catalog has autocompleted the word that is being typed, and even proposes several alternatives. We will discuss this further.

Figure 3-5. Simple search for data analytics

Once the search is launched, another set of calculations takes place: namely, what hits will be returned and in what order they will appear in the search result. Again, this is in no way a simple procedure, but a result of the data catalog matching several properties of the query with the crawled IT landscape, along with exactly who you are (the data catalog remembers you).

In simple search, you can also perform queries of slightly higher complexity, adding more values by combining them with operators. You can, for example, search for sensitive assets in an HR domain (defined as capability in this case), writing the following query, also shown in Figure 3-6:

Capability: HR AND ClassificationOfSensitivity: Sensitive

Nevertheless, using the search bar quickly gets a little unmanageable when trying to write long search statements, as parts of your search disappear to the left. Therefore, you can click on the advanced button and simply get a bigger box to write your search in. You will see what that looks like in "Complex Search."

Also, data catalogs can have a special feature that enables simple search only in the glossaries. It's usually accessed by the pile of books icon on the right side of the search bar. This search feature works just like simple search, except it only searches for glossary terms.

Figure 3-6. Searching for sensitive assets in HR

Now, let's look at how simple search actually works.

Simple search is programmed to help you behind the scenes. To work at maximum capacity, simple search is powered by a wide range of mathematical procedures. You will never discover how these procedures work as an end user, as it will be part of the intellectual property of the data catalog provider. Nevertheless, you would immediately discover the absence of those mathematical procedures. Without the things going on behind the scenes, simple search would give you nothing but a big mess of meaningless noise, with completely irrelevant search results regardless of what you were searching for. Many of your attempts to do simple search wouldn't even result in hits if you, for example, misspelled a glossary term or couldn't remember an old project name and guessed wrong—even if you came close.

A well-programmed simple search will subtly help you by correcting your queries, suggesting other queries, and even remembering your search habits. Some of the technology features that do this are:

- Autocomplete
- String matching
- Synonym ring
- Thesaurus
- Ontology
- Search behavior

Although these features work behind the scenes, you need to know them, because you can influence them and thereby improve your simple search.

Autocomplete is a live suggestion for endings of words as you type them, just like you see in Figure 3-5. It draws on the glossaries in the data catalog. So the more you enrich your glossaries and the more you search, the better predictions you get. It can also be enriched with natural language processing and machine learning.

String matching (also referred to as *fuzzy logic*) searches for all the values that come closest to the search that is being performed. String matching not only deals with misspellings, it can also take into account the many alternative versions of acknowledged ways of writing, for example, names (e.g., Dostoevsky/Dostoievsky), as well as conventions for digits (e.g., different ways of writing dates, such as 20-05-2022 and May 20th 2022) and acronyms (e.g., NATO/OTAN) and similar.

Synonym ring refers to a group of data elements that are considered semantically equivalent for the purposes of information retrieval. You might have seen this when shopping online and the website suggests other products that might interest you. A ring of synonyms can also be relevant in a data catalog. It could be in cases where projects are renamed or when they are reignited or refocused. In global companies with product names that vary between sales regions, such as is the case in pharma, a synonym ring will also be very useful in a data catalog simple search, just like product alternatives on the open web.

Thesaurus is the broadening of synonym rings to the global glossary, as discussed in Chapter 2. It's the entire cluster of glossary terms surrounding the value you searched for, which will affect the selection and ranking of hits in your search result.

Ontology: if your data catalog is based on a knowledge graph, then nodes close to the node you are searching for would be ranked high in the search result, also.

 The better you build your thesaurus, and the more you use it to organize your data, the better a simple search feature you get.

Search behavior is when the data catalog simple search remembers your search habits (what you searched, what you ultimately selected) and those results influence your later search results. In the best data catalogs, your search behavior is taken into account by the algorithm performing the search when your search results are selected and ranked.

Another way to search the data catalog for the information you need is by browsing.

Browsing

We've all browsed through shelves with books, collections of old-school vinyls, or through massive amounts of pictures in Instagram. You don't really know when to stop, and you might not be entirely sure what you are searching for. Browsing is when you're scanning through content without meticulously looking at all the details of each element in that flow.

In the data catalog in Hugin & Munin, you browse by clicking the magnifying glass. Under the magnifying glass, your domain opens downward, in more and more specific subdomains. You can always browse up again, and then down again. Below the most specific subdomains are your data sources and finally your assets (see Figure 3-7), from `Customer Management`, to `Customer Information Management`, further down into `Customer Profile Management`, where you can find data sources with assets.

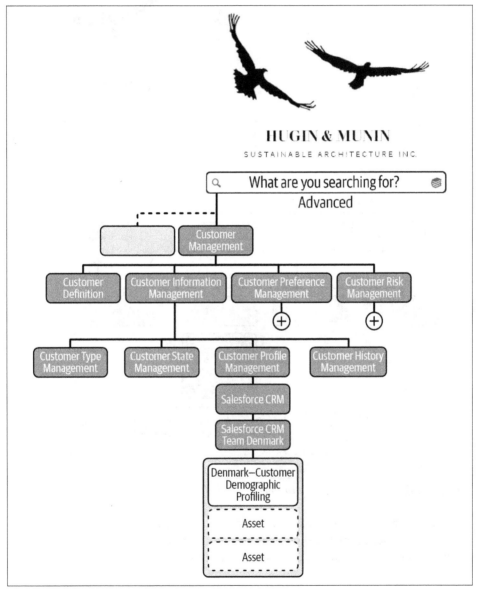

Figure 3-7. Browsing vertically in domains

From this point on, you can browse sideways in your assets data lineage. This enables you to see how your asset has traveled from the source upstream, and how it continues further downstream, as depicted in Figure 3-8.

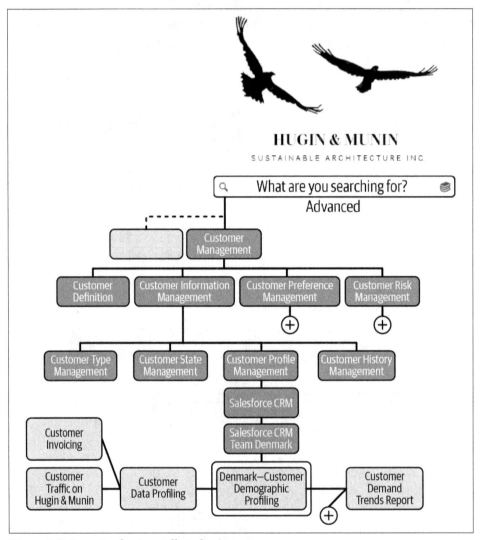

Figure 3-8. Browsing horizontally in lineage

You can also browse relationally. By doing that, you move associatively from your asset toward other assets that hold data related to some of the data in the asset that was your point of departure. You can see this illustrated in Figure 3-9.

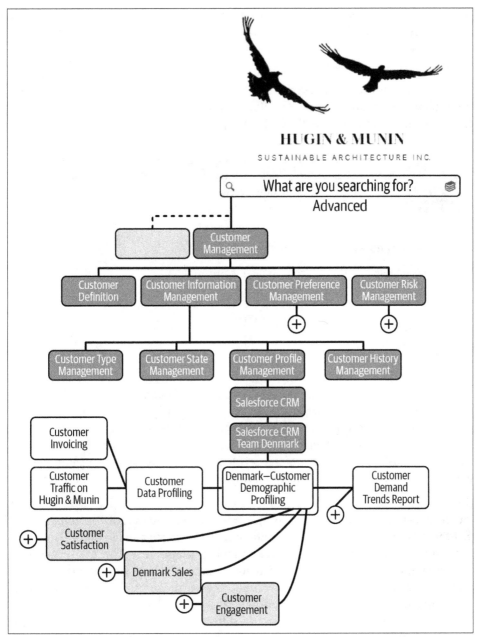

Figure 3-9. Browsing relationally in graph

If you have organized your data perfectly vertically, horizontally, and relationally, you have the possibility to browse that organization again in all three directions. You can browse your data landscape horizontally in domains and subdomains. At any given point, you can continue browsing vertically, following the lineage of a given asset in a domain upstream or downstream, outside of the domain where the asset is placed. Or, if you want, you can continue to browse relationally, in elements that are associatively connected to your asset.

As you can see, if you organize your data to the most complete level in the data catalog, what you get is an easy, seamless flow in your browsing experience across all the data in all directions in your entire IT landscape.

 Browse puts you in a position of perfect discovery for things you were not necessarily looking for but which could be very useful now that you know that they exist.

Now let's look at how browsing actually works.

Browsing is enabled by three technological features:

- Push/pull
- Data lineage
- Knowledge graphs

Push/pull enables vertical browsing, since a prerequisite for pushing/pulling data is the creation of domains, as discussed in Chapter 2. Domains are where you push or pull your data source and store its assets. But this also makes it the feature that allows you to perform vertical browsing, since domains can have subdomains that can have even narrower subdomains and so on. Only at the lowest, most-specific level do you set up your push/pulls, and therefore, this location also creates a vertical browsable structure above itself that can help you navigate in the data of your organization.

Data lineage is horizontal browsing of how your asset travels from data source to data source, and—ideally—how it transforms underway. Technologically, what happens is that the data catalog, as it crawls the data source, can create a map of how data assets inside it travel between that data source and other data sources. This is a very diverse task, given the enormous number of data tools out there. Every data catalog has a specific focus in their data lineage feature, and no data catalog is ideal for all scenarios. Therefore, many data catalog providers partner with data lineage solutions to provide high-quality lineage. There are at least 14 different ways to approach data lineage,[5] and you should not expect all those to be present in one solution—not even close.

---

5 Bonnie K. O'Neil and Lowell Fryman, *The Data Catalog: Sherlock Holmes Data Sleuthing for Analytics* (Basking Ridge, NJ: Technics Publications, 2020), 196–97. Albeit in my view, of these 14, some must be regarded as semantic relations or knowledge graph relations.

As you will see in Chapters 4 and 5, data lineage is a very useful feature for both governance and analytics stakeholders.

Knowledge graphs are relational browsing. Knowledge graphs are not lineage, as they do not depict how data travels, but how data is conceptually related and how it is organized. Knowledge graphs consist of entities (nodes) and relationships (edges) between the entities. Nodes can be terms, persons, assets, data sources, domains—whatever is in the data catalog. The knowledge graph is an extremely powerful tool. It is a quintessential feature behind the best and most-used search engines on the web, but knowledge graphs go back several decades as technology.[6] The reason why it is so powerful is that it allows you to relate all your assets as you want and search for them as you please.[7] The latter is the most desirable for your company, as it best captures the vastness of data and the connections between it. Furthermore, knowledge graphs can be made from manual activity of relating nodes, or, even more powerfully, automatically, as you scan data sources, based on machine learning and natural language processing.

And now, we will look at the kinds of search that require the most from your end users' side but will deliver fantastic results if they master it.

Complex search

The first thing you need to know about complex search is that it really is complex. To truly master complex search, you must be cautious about two elements from DCQL: (1) you must carefully use the correct syntax in the query language—if you misspell your operators or values, then your query won't run; and (2) even more difficult, you must be very aware of the semantics in your search. Are the assets in your statement actually the ones you are looking for? Did you reverse the logic of the Boolean operators? Was your grouping of values correct? You need to be sure of that. That said, don't be afraid to fire off wrong queries; just pay attention to what happens, analyze the result, and eventually adjust and search again. Unlike when searching in data, searching for data with wrong, heavy queries has no computational cost.

The second thing you need to know is that complex search is in fact very simple. Not for the user, but for the data catalog as software. It is easy to deliver a complex search capability from the data catalog provider's side—a substantially smaller part of the technologies behind simple search are necessary to perform complex search.

---

6 Claudio Gutierrez and Juan F. Sequeda, "Knowledge Graphs" (*https://oreil.ly/uwLs8*), *Communications of the ACM* 64, no. 3 (March 2021): 96–104.

7 Mark Needham and Amy E. Hodler, *Graph Algorithms: Practical Examples in Apache Spark and Neo4j* (Sebastopol, CA: O'Reilly, 2019).

There is a yin-yang relationship between simplicity and complexity in search, a *complexity of simplicity and simplicity of complexity*. Simple search may appear very easy to you, but it takes computational efforts. Complex search may, on the other hand, appear complex to you, but that is because there has been only a little computational effort.

Figure 3-10 shows a complex search. The search combines one or more asset stewards with one or more generic data sources and with one or more glossary terms from taxonomies. Finally, pay close attention to the use of the asterisk (*), which allows multiple endings.

Figure 3-10. Complex search for Power BI or Qlik Sense assets owned by Kris, Handan, or Peter dealing with sales in the United States

You may ask yourself: "If complex search is so hard for me as an end user, compared to simple search, why should I do it at all? Why not just stick to simple search?" It's because sometimes simple search simply doesn't give you the answers you want, in relation to what you are searching for. We will discuss this in Chapter 4.

With complex search, what you see is what you get. There is nothing going on behind the scenes, as in simple search. You have to write the entire search query, and you have to get syntax and semantics right. Accordingly, building complex search relies on technologies at a very low level of complexity. The data catalog has to understand and execute the operators on the values you apply in the search—that's it.

Complex search will typically yield a long list of hits, and you will need to peruse the results and assess if any of them fit your needs. You shouldn't skim through the results and focus on just the ones that happen to catch your eye, because you might miss something; that is *browsing*. Instead, you will be *perusing* the search results. *Perusing* is to read something in a thorough or careful way. In the most intense hunts after data in complex search, you will be perusing the search results returned.

We have looked at search from many different angles, but now, let's discuss the limitations of what you can search in a data catalog.

Searching for Everything?

The dream of searching for everything is as old as human civilization itself. But what about data in a data catalog? Can you search everything in a data catalog?

No, the logical limit of what you can search is the IRQL of your data catalog. If your IRQL does not contain the option of searching for, say, a data owner, then that search is simply not possible to perform. That's why you want a deep, well-structured IRQL to support search beyond simple search.

Certain catalogs, however, enable you to search beyond the IRQL, and in two ways:

- Searching in data
- Searching for all metadata (all the data in the data catalog)

Searching in data. Certain data catalogs allow for assets to be accessed via or sampled in the data catalog. When you have searched for and found your data asset, via searches in the metadata represented in the data catalog, you can continue, and search *in* the data, either in or via the data catalog.

Searching for all metadata. In some cases, you also have the opportunity to search all the metadata in the data catalog, beyond what is defined in the IRQL of the data catalog. This is the case for knowledge graph–based data catalogs, as discussed in Chapter 2.

Now, let's look at the mechanics at play when we search.

The Mechanics of Search

By now, you know why you search in a data catalog, you know what you are searching for, and you know how to do it. The final section in this chapter is devoted to the mechanics of search. As you are about to discover, the mechanics of search will help you understand when to apply which kind of search for data. It's a dimension that you need to take into account when you are assessing what your information need is and how you should formulate or perform a search to meet that need.

Recall and Precision

Imagine that you discover a red area on the upper side of your left hand. It itches, and the skin in that area looks dry. You book an appointment with your doctor. Once you are face-to-face with your doctor, you ask her: "Is this eczema?"

We all intuitively think that two things can happen from this moment on. The doctor can say either "yes" or "no." But in fact, four things can happen because, besides diagnosing correctly, the doctor may diagnose wrongly. The doctor can say "yes" but be wrong, or say "no" and be wrong.

Being diagnosed with a medical condition is referred to as being *positive*. Diagnosed as not having the medical condition is called being *negative*. And accordingly, getting positively diagnosed without having the medical condition is called *false positive*. Likewise, if you have the medical condition but are diagnosed as negative, you are a *false negative*.

Not only is this true in medicine when diagnosing patients, it's also true when calculating the effectiveness of search in data catalogs. Here's how.

In Figure 3-11 you can see what is called a confusion matrix. In it, you can see that the confusion matrix groups *true positives* and *false negatives* as all the actual positives. And it groups the false positives and true negatives as all the actual negatives. Further, just like patients in the case of medicine, you can see that, despite how you search in a data catalog, you will have *true positives*, hits that are relevant, and *false positives*, hits that are not relevant. There will also be a series of hits that are not found in your search, even though they are relevant; these are the *false negatives*. And there will be a remaining group of hits you did not get that are *true negatives*—those are the hits that are correctly not part of your search result.

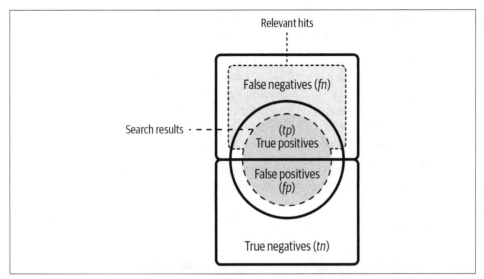

Figure 3-11. Confusion matrix with search results and relevant hits

Recall and precision are the most fundamental mechanics of search. No search you will ever conduct escapes the confusion matrix: some hits will be retrieved without being relevant, and some will not be retrieved, even though they were relevant.

The confusion matrix is used to represent many mathematical formulas that go deep into the inner workings of classification (*https://oreil.ly/ppWCK*)—including for search in a data catalog. You do not need to know all the formulas at play in the data catalog that are based on the confusion matrix.[8] But you do need to know about *recall* and *precision*, because you must take them into account when you search.

Recall is calculated by dividing the number of true positives (*tp*) by the sum of the number of true positives (*tp*) and the number of false negatives (*fn*). Metrics must be put in place to calculate recall or make an approximate assessment of recall.

$$Recall = \frac{tp}{tp + fn}$$

Recall measures how many relevant hits you retrieve in your search—in relation to the total number of relevant hits in your data catalog. The complex search function ranks recall highest, as you typically want all results of even just potential relevance to what you are looking for when you formulate long, complex queries in your data

---

8 But a mathematical understanding of these laws can lead to improved search features both in your data catalog and beyond; see G. G. Chowdhury, *Introduction to Modern Information Retrieval* (New York: Neal-Schuman Publishers, 2010), chap. 9.

catalog. Basically, you are looking for assets of just the slightest relevance in your entire data catalog when you are maximizing recall.

Recall is often difficult to calculate because you have only approximate ideas about how many false negatives are actually in your data catalog. Therefore, if you believe that your search results are not providing enough recall, assess a relative number of false negatives and do the calculation. Either you work on improving the ratio to around 0.75 (see Chapter 4, "Flexible Simple Search," on how) or, as an alternative, browse the catalog to evaluate if your assessment is correct.

Precision is calculated by dividing the number of true positives (*tp*) by the sum of the number of true positives (*tp*) and the number of false positives (*fp*).

$$Precision = \frac{tp}{tp + fp}$$

Precision is always easy to calculate, because you only evaluate the search result and not what you have not found. It's therefore also fair to strive for very high precision and aim for 0.9. It's also easy to improve, because you can modify search and easily measure if your precision improves.

The simple search function ranks precision highest, as you typically want just a few, exact hits, which helps you in what you are doing right now. Contrary to recall, you cannot expect to find everything of potential relevance when maximizing precision. Pertinent information in your data catalog is left out when you strive for precision, and that's OK—you are not looking for each and every potentially relevant search hit in the catalog, just for whatever gets you going with what you want to do.

You need to know recall and precision because you cannot search in a way that maximizes both at the same time. So if you strive for precision in your search, be aware that you will not receive a search result that caters to recall. And vice versa, if you are searching for every potential asset of relevance, you will not get a search result with very high precision.

In "Simple search" on page 59, I described mechanisms that improve simple search. These mechanisms are all mathematical calculations taking place behind the scenes to make simple search powerful and easy for the end user. Basically, all these mechanisms serve the purpose of precision.

When you are doing simple searches, you're aiming for precision. Don't expect recall, and don't try to obtain it. Take a look at Figure 4-1. It is one word. It results in one—or a few—relevant search hits. That's precision.

In "Complex search" on page 67, I described mechanisms that improve complex search. These mechanisms are based on DCQL, and they are not taking place behind the scenes but are performed by the end user, either as a query language or as point-and-click options, combined with drag-and-drop tools to formulate complex queries. Basically, these mechanisms serve the purpose of recall.

> When you are doing complex searches, you're aiming for recall. Don't expect precision, and don't try to obtain it. Take a look at Figure 4-5. It's a long statement. It results in many, many hits, of which a lot may be relevant. That's recall.

In Chapter 2, I discussed exhaustivity and specificity. Think of nicely curated assets, with many glossary terms assigned to them from exhaustive glossaries, so that the asset has a high degree of specificity. Now, think of this in relation to recall and precision. Searching for those nicely curated assets is possible by using a high level of exhaustivity in glossaries, which increases recall and decreases precision.

Zipf's Law

There is an inevitable problem built into the type of data catalog that crawls: the more you crawl, the more your crawled metadata loses its meaning; it might be depicting your assets correctly, but only in ways that group more and more different assets with the same kinds of metadata, even though the assets have little or nothing in common. Imagine tables in many different data sources that all have a column called *Efficiency*, *Result*, or *Score*. There is nothing wrong with these column names; they depict the values in them. However, the columns in the different tables in the different data sources have absolutely no relation to each other. But, when crawled by the data catalog, they are all part of the search result if you search for, e.g., *Result*, even though they do not have anything in common. The more data sources you crawl, the more this will happen.

The problem is rooted in Zipf's law—you need to know it, to avoid it.

Zipf's law is named after George Kingsley Zipf (1902–1950).[9] The law states that the frequency, *f*, of words are, more or less, inversely proportional to their rank, *r*.

$$Frequency(f) \propto \frac{1}{rank(r)}$$

---

9 Although he didn't really invent it and it isn't really a law. See Erez Aiden and Jean-Baptiste Michel, *Uncharted: Big Data as a Lens on Human Culture* (New York: Riverhead Books, 2013), 249, Zipf's law.

For example, the most common word in English is "the," and it occurs once for every 10 words in a typical text. The second most common word is "of," and it occurs once for every 20 words in a typical text—and so it goes. The bigger the body of text, the more accurate Zipf's law is. Zipf argued that two opposing forces compete in our language: *unification* (general words with many meanings) and *diversification* (specific words with precise meanings).

Zipf's law is also at play in search.[10] Here, it has been demonstrated that Zipf's unification equals *description*, meaning a complete description of an asset. And diversification equals *discrimination*, the ability to distinguish assets from each other.

The problem is that more and more data is pulled or pushed into the data catalog from table and column names, folders and files. And Zipf's law just gets more and more true the more times the data catalog does this: the number of names that strive toward description, and not diversification, will increase as the number of data sources increases in the data catalog. The same words will inevitably have more and more meanings. And then suddenly you are in a situation where, say, hundreds of tables hold data about *Efficiency*, *Result*, or *Score*. And that may be true; these tables are correctly described with the crawled metadata. But they are not discriminated: you cannot tell one from the other—you don't know which is relevant in what context.

This is where glossary terms come into the picture. To counteract Zipf's law, you simply need to tag your assets with glossary terms to make your assets stand out and be distinguishable from other assets that hold the same kind of crawled metadata even though they stem from different parts of the business and are really about different things.

For example, the above-mentioned tables about *Score* could be tagged with terms such as "wood durability," "customer satisfaction," or "employee performance" so that they become distinguishable from one another.

 You should not interpret Zipf's law as a reason to do Master Data Management (MDM) in data catalogs. That's unnecessary, in fact, in a data catalog context; metadata is what you need to do to improve search.

---

10 David C. Blair, "The Challenge of Commercial Document Retrieval, Part I" (*https://oreil.ly/Su4iI*), *Information Processing & Management* 38, no. 2 (March 2002): 273–91.

Serendipity

Serendipity is when you find good stuff you weren't looking for. If you have ever wondered what Google's "I'm Feeling Lucky" button is all about: it's serendipity. Go to Google. Type in a search term and then click the "I'm Feeling Lucky" button. It'll automatically take you to one of the top search results for that term. It might be exactly what you're looking for, but it might not. It might lead you down a different path to get to an answer other than the one you expected. You might even discover new things along the way. That's serendipity.

 Compared to just browsing search results, serendipity is something that can be built into the ranking mechanism. At its best, serendipity distracts the user with what they weren't searching for, but what they would be interested in anyway.

Data catalogs, too, should offer serendipity. Here, serendipity is finding potentially interesting assets in unplanned ways. Serendipity is a key enabler for the high usage of your data catalog: users will be naturally drawn to the data catalog if they know they will discover surprising and useful assets when they search in it. Think of serendipity as a magnetic force: the stronger it is, the more it pulls users into the data catalog and the more value it generates.

Serendipity consists of four elements: *insight, experience, luck,* and *coincidence.* You simply need to maximize each to maximize serendipity.

Serendipity: insight + experience + luck + coincidence[11]

The more your data catalog takes into account these four elements, the higher the serendipity. The data sources and how their assets are described and tagged must reflect the *insight* of your users, in the sense of what the users know, to appeal to them. Also, the *experience* of your users must be put in play: in this case, the users may not necessarily have great insight about an asset but simply know by experience that it exists—and so being exposed to that creates curiosity. A user—say from HR—may discover an asset that describes some experiments from the R&D department that the user has heard of, and confronted with that asset, the user could be tempted to take a closer look at it. So, experience means that search results should also take into account not only what people know due to their field of expertise, but the haphazard experience they gather by being surrounded by other coworkers in a given context. Finally, the

---

11 The "formula" for serendipity has been put forward as a conceptual way to understand the elements that constitute serendipity in the Danish science forum Videnskab.dk (*https://oreil.ly/clRsp*) (website in Danish). For further reading on serendipity, see Robert K. Merton (*https://oreil.ly/trQkL*) and Elinor Barber (*https://oreil.ly/E0rYV*), *The Travels and Adventures of Serendipity: A Study in Sociological Semantics and the Sociology of Science* (Princeton, NJ: Princeton University Press, 2004).

search mechanisms inside the data catalog must take into account *luck* and *coincidence*—luck is not the same as coincidence! Luck is, for example, when a query that the user is not sure will work happens to return useful assets. Coincidence is when the user discovers something that was out of scope of what the user was searching for. You could argue that serendipity is simply coincidence, but it's not; the other elements—insight, experience, and luck—play a role in increasing serendipity to its maximum performance.

You can encourage the likelihood of serendipity by fine-tuning glossaries and descriptions of assets. You can further improve it by using certain mechanisms, such as having the data catalog remember your search history—that would result in a mechanism providing more search results of potential relevance to you.

 Serendipity has an evil twin: zemblanity. It's when you find bad stuff you absolutely weren't looking for. Social media is full of zemblanity, of evil, unnecessary comments about—and actions against—other people. Your data catalog will not suffer substantially from zemblanity, as it is a professional tool and people accordingly keep a friendly tone—most of the time. But it can occur, since a data catalog is a collaborative platform that normally offers debate about the quality and potential use of assets. Zemblanity in a data catalog is when you would, for example, stumble upon a vicious, unjust comment about yourself or a close colleague, say in a case where your asset descriptions were misinterpreted to suggest that your work was poor or even amateurish. Watch out for zemblanity—keep it out of your data catalog at all costs!

Summary

In this chapter we discussed why, what, and how you search in a data catalog, as well as the mechanics of search:

- Why do you search a data catalog? Because it enables data discovery. Data discovery starts with finding the best data sources.
- What do you search in a data catalog? In a data catalog, you are not searching in data, but for data.
- How do you search a data catalog? You use a combination of query language commands, operators, and clickable filters. You can use simple search, browsing, and complex search:
  - Simple search is simple for you, but complex behind the scenes. It provides search results based on how you have previously searched. It also corrects your queries and makes suggestions.

— Browse search can be vertical, horizontal, and relational. Vertical browsing is based on domains, and on the most specific level pushes or pulls data sources into the data catalog. Horizontal browsing is based on data lineage and displays how data travels across systems. Relational browsing is based in graph technology and maps how data is conceptually connected.

— Complex search is complex for you but simple behind the scenes. It requires you to master an IRQL and apply it when you search. You need to take into account syntax and semantics of your searches, so that your hits reflect what you are actually looking for.

- The mechanics of search describe the most basic mathematics behind search:

— Recall and precision enable you to measure how well your complex and simple searches work.

— Zipf's law explains why you can't rely on crawled metadata. The more you crawl, the more your crawled metadata loses meaning.

— Serendipity is the capability to find useful assets you weren't looking for.

Next up will be an aha moment: in the following chapter, you'll see search applied for the data in your company.

CHAPTER 4

Apply Search: From Simple to Advanced Patterns

In the previous chapter, we discussed how search works in a data catalog and how understanding the search mechanics can improve how you search and thus drive up the value of your data catalog. You have to remember that search is dependent on how well you organize the data in your data catalog. Even if you compose the perfect query statement for what you need, the search will struggle to return anything if the data catalog has poor metadata.

This brings us to how to apply search. Applying search is a craft that is different from understanding the technology itself. First of all, when searching for data, you need to search like a librarian who is trained in searching *for* data, and not like a data scientist who is trained to search *in* data. With a librarian's mindset, you will find creative ways to unlock search features. Simple search can be used in a variety of ways that increase and decrease precision in order to search more broadly or for only very few hits. Browsing enables navigation in data and understanding its context—and an additional benefit is that this context can be used to refine both simple and complex search. And just as simple search can be used in many different ways, so can complex search.

What you will learn in this chapter is only the beginning. You will need to further adapt and refine applied search so that it matches the language and purpose of your company.

Search Like Librarians—Not Like Data Scientists

Data scientists excel at analyzing data—from small to massive datasets, they have the tools and mindset to search in the data to extract the findings they need. That's their superpower. Searching for the data for them to work on, however, can be a real challenge because the skills that make them very good at searching in data don't necessarily apply to searching for data. As you'll recall from Chapter 3, there's a significant difference between searching for data versus searching in data.

Librarians, on the other hand, are very good at locating all kinds of material under the sun— books, periodicals, papers, everything! If you ask for it, they could probably search for it and find it. And their superpowers also include searching for data and knowing what data you need.

Unlike data science, which has gained importance only in the last decades, library and information science (LIS) has existed for hundreds of years, with as many years perfecting the art of organizing knowledge and searching for it.

To search as a librarian means, first and foremost, being good at assessing an information need, because the information need determines how you search for data. *Information need* was coined as a term in 1962 by Robert S. Taylor as the way we ask questions to reference databases.[1]

Your information need can be big or small. Ask yourself whether you are searching for:

- Everything
- A few good things
- The sole right thing
- A thing you need again[2]

Your information need determines how you search for data, as needs express different sizes and intentions.

Everything entails complex search—and you're aiming for high recall at the expense of precision. But you can do this in many different ways, as you will see later in this chapter.

A few good things is an information need that is not that clear cut. You can be searching for either relatively high recall or relatively high precision, but not both.

The sole right thing, as the name alludes, aims at finding just one asset, or one precisely defined set of assets. Therefore, these searches strive for precision.

---

1 Robert S. Taylor, "The Process of Asking Questions," *American Documentation* 13, no. 4 (October 1962): 391–96.

2 Information needs can be grouped differently; this grouping is from Louis Rosenfeld et al., *Information Architecture: For the Web and Beyond* (Sebastopol, CA: O'Reilly, 2015), 45.

Finally, *a thing you need again* relies on assets that you already know. It also strives for precision, but it's less difficult to search for than *the sole right thing*.

What you need to keep in mind is that searching for data in metadata repositories like a data catalog can be a long process (just as Taylor already pointed out in 1962). So don't get impatient. We are used to being able to google everything, but that's simple search playing tricks on you. Searching for data is not always like that; it can take many steps before you find what you are searching for, and that's OK. You may need to make adjustments to searches, both of the translations of what is intended with a search into how the specific IRQL of the system works and, from that point on, what terms are included, which of those are subsequently excluded or modified, and so on, in a multiple-step long search for the most relevant and valuable hits. This means that search is not just a matter of translating *one* information need into *one* search. The process is way more subtle, and it takes experience.

Searching for data is like driving a car. Sometimes, you're just out for a short ride to pick up stuff. Occasionally, you're on a long, tiresome road on a straight line. Once in a while, you cross mountains with endless sharp corners, the feeling of vertigo, up and down, until you reach the destination. Or it happens that you go one place only to discover that you need to go to a second place, then a third place, before you can return home with the things you were out to get. Sometimes you find yourself in areas with no rules, sometimes the traffic is overwhelming, sometimes the roads are old and full of holes. And sometimes, you just go as fast as you possibly can because it's fun.

Librarians combine all sorts of methods and techniques when they search—you should, too. The next sections will go over some of the most commonly applied search patterns. Although they each can work fine in isolation, they work best when combined.

Search Patterns

Have you ever noticed that how you search depends on what you're searching for? In this section, I will discuss typical patterns of applied search. You will see how recall, precision, serendipity, exhaustivity, specificity, and other concepts are at play when you search.

All the search patterns are listed in Table 4-1, with a search name, search type, a short description, and the search's relative level of precision and recall. Note that precision and recall are not applicable to browsing.

Notice how the search type softens the distinction between simple search and complex search.

Table 4-1. Search patterns

Search name	Search type	Description	Precision	Recall
Basic simple search	Simple search	A few precise hits and a lot of noise	High	Low
Detailed simple search	Simple combinatorial search	Slowly formulated simple search, because the search must be precisely formulated	High	Low
Flexible simple search	Simple combinatorial search	Truncated search that eases and broadens a simple search	Low	High
Range search	Complex combinatorial search	Range search that allows retrieval of assets between two values	High	Low
Block search	Complex combinatorial search	Combination of selected terms to depict a topic	Low	High
Statement search	Complex combinatorial search	Long statement of precise conditions assets must meet	High	Low
Glossary browsing	Browse search	Lookups after specific word results in lists of words in the glossary that can be browsed	—	—
Domain browsing	Browse search	Domains as explained in Chapter 3	—	—
Lineage browsing	Browse search	Lineage as explained in Chapter 3	—	—
Graph browsing	Browse search	Graphs as explained in Chapter 3	—	—

Let's talk about each one.

Basic Simple Search

In general, your casual searches during a typical workday are probably basic simple searches with a couple words in the search bar. You do these kinds of searches when you are not aiming for anything near total recall—you just want something good, fast. What matters in this type of search is the hit at the top of the search results. That hit, seen in isolation from the rest of the search result, must be a perfect precision hit. Anything below that top hit doesn't matter.

Simple searches use plain-language search terms and not query language. *Basic simple search* is the least complicated kind of search you can do, as it consists of only one or two plain-language search terms, such as "good weather" or "summer."

For example, let's say that a sales rep for Hugin & Munin assigned to Sweden wants to find the latest, most relevant sales BI report for their area. They might do a basic simple search for sales, as shown in Figure 4-1. The sales rep, being an average end user, expects the top result to be the exact thing they were looking for. If it's not, then they move on to more-complex search patterns to try to find what they are looking for.

Because simple search takes into account all of the technologies mentioned in Chapter 3, such as prediction, fuzzy logic, and history of search behavior, it does a good job of figuring out what the average user wants.

Figure 4-1. Simple search for sales

The sales rep will expect to get the latest, most relevant sales BI report for the area the user is a sales rep in. This reflects the most precise, relevant hit on top, based on who the user is, what kind of data most interests the user, and how the user has previously searched.

 If your data catalog is based on a knowledge graph, expect to have a very powerful simple search feature. Search results will enlighten you as to the business contexts of a given asset and be ranked with high precision. This is, for example, the case with Google's Knowledge Graph (*https://oreil.ly/Tynyn*).

Basic simple search will be the only way many end users will use the data catalog. This search engine–like experience creates an impression of ambient findability—but that's not what it is. It's the easiest kind of search. It will offer end users precision at the expense of recall. Users will be able to find the one right thing at the top of the search results.

 It's common for data catalog providers to demonstrate basic simple search as the only way to search in sales material—it's often this exact way of searching that handles whatever users are searching for. Nevertheless, it's impossible for this kind of search to deliver on all information needs. But other kinds of searches are more difficult and time-consuming, and therefore rarely promoted.

Detailed Simple Search

Sometimes you are looking for one type of thing and only that—and you know how to express it, if you concentrate. This is a relatively simple search that is not fast, because you have to get your search syntax right; it's detailed. You might even have to do a couple of initial searches to test that everything works as intended.

Detailed simple search is when you need to use a bit of query language to formulate your search statement. This search is slow, because it relies on users to type exact values, which requires attention, and this slows down the search process. The search type is a simple combinatorial search, because it's a relatively simple search statement that is combined with only one Boolean operator. If you take a look at the spectrum of search in Figure 3-4, we are moving away from *easy* toward *difficult*.

In Hugin & Munin, our fictional sustainable architecture company, end users make use of their well-curated global glossary, which allows them to search in finely granulated words, e.g., for types of wood: heartwood, spruce, pine, and so on. Words for wood in the global glossary are the standard English names for kinds of wood combined with their Latin name. Let's say you want to search for assets with the steward John Miller that hold data about ash trees from the global glossary, like this:

GlobalGlossary:Ash Fraxinus AND AssetSteward:John Miller

It's possible to type this in the simple search view without completely losing the overview of the search typed inside the simple search bar, as in Figure 4-2.

Figure 4-2. Detailed simple search

This search gathers all the assets with the global glossary term "Ash Fraxinus" that have "John Miller" as an asset steward. In this search, the user would perhaps need to determine the right way to express the type of wood in the global glossary before performing the search. This search will take some time to build but will deliver precise results, as only the assets with the distinct characteristics of the search are returned. So, unlike *basic simple search*, all hits are relevant here, precision is high and recall is low, and the search itself takes a little time to create.

You can also loosen the syntax and move away from a detailed simple search pattern into a flexible search pattern. In that case, simple searches are not totally precise but become relatively fast.

Flexible Simple Search

You may also sometimes need to perform searches that are imprecise and that will require some perusing through the search results to find the assets you had in mind.

That's *flexible simple search*, and it's a little faster to write than detailed simple search because it depends less on exact syntax; you don't need to know the exact values in your query statement. Flexible simple search is also a simple combinatorial search, but it allows for a larger set of search hits and a higher recall, at the expense of precision.

For example, a group of Hugin & Munin employees in the communications department need to know what kinds of wood the company uses in order to include some details in a press release. They heard that the info is in a CSV file. They don't know how the asset is described in the catalog except that it contains data on wood and it's a CSV file. They might search the following, shown in Figure 4-3:

FreeGlossary:*Wood* AND FormatDefault:.csv

Figure 4-3. Flexible simple search

This search results in all assets that represent CSV files and that have folksonomy terms with the word "wood" in them, but truncated on both sides so that the results are open to all combinations with wood. So, for example, free glossary terms such as "wooden floor," "beautiful wood," "woods," and so on are automatically included in the search.

This type of search will provide high recall and therefore compromise on precision. And that's the point: the end user does not know how to search this in a way that delivers complete precision and must therefore aim for higher recall to retrieve a group of assets wherein the asset is located.

Range Search

Sometimes you have to search for something between two points, such as dates or anything that holds organizational logic in serial numbers.

That's done with *range search*. It's a more refined complex combinatorial search type, which uses one or more Boolean operators and at least two values that establish a range.

For example, if you were looking for a given set of hypotheses that were tested sometime around when particular projects were carried out, you might search research projects like this:

> RES.100.7.1003 AND < RES.100.7.1837

It can also be room numbers on floor plans, equipment, and so on.

For example, a project team in Hugin & Munin wants to analyze all pictures of heartwood between November 2012 and February 2018. They search like this, shown in Figure 4-4:

AssetTypeFree:Picture of heartwood AND (< 01.31.2018 AND > 10.31.2012)

That search returns all hits that refer to pictures of heartwood in the specified period of time.

Figure 4-4. Range search

Block Search

Say an unhappy customer has decided to file a lawsuit against Hugin & Munin. The house Hugin & Munin built for him has cracks in the facade, and the customer argues the wood that the house is built of is not solid enough.

Block search is a very comprehensive complex combinatorial search, where you are searching for an entire topic. Generally, a lot of different things and words are at play in such a search, and you order those in related groups as blocks, hence the name *block search*.

The lawyers in Hugin & Munin start their due diligence by searching. Using their basic training in DCQL, they search the data catalog for reports and test data that examine the hardiness of different kinds of wood in the company's own constructions. They combine a large selection of words to maximize recall—they have to get every single potentially relevant asset, with the consequence of having little precision, so they expect to be perusing quite a lot through the search results. They search as follows, shown in Figure 4-5:

(DomainTerm:((Pine OR Ash OR Beech OR Oak OR Wood) NOT Linden) OR FreeTerm:Wood OR GlobalTerm:(Pine Pinus OR Ash Fraxinus OR Beech Fagus OR Oak Quercus) NOT Linden Tilia) AND DomainTerm:(Hardiness OR Solidity OR Endurance OR Resilience)

Figure 4-5. Block search

The search results will show assets that have one or more combinations of terms for *wood* and terms for *hardiness*.

The search consists of domain glossary terms from different domains that describe types of wood in standard English. The assets must have one or more of these words, unless the asset holds the next value, the free glossary term *wood*, or one or more of the global glossary terms for wood—as the word "wood" is not a term found in the global glossary. It can also hold a mix of these words. If one or more of all these criteria are met, then these must be matched with the domain glossary terms for hardiness.

But not all lawyers have been trained in the data catalog's query language, and they get a little dizzy trying to control the syntax while at the same time focusing on the semantics. Therefore, some of the lawyers just use the search builder. They enter the search builder from the advanced search field. The search builder allows end users to formulate their search with point-and-click options, which removes the stress of checking the syntax and focuses only on the semantics. You can see the search builder in Figure 4-6.

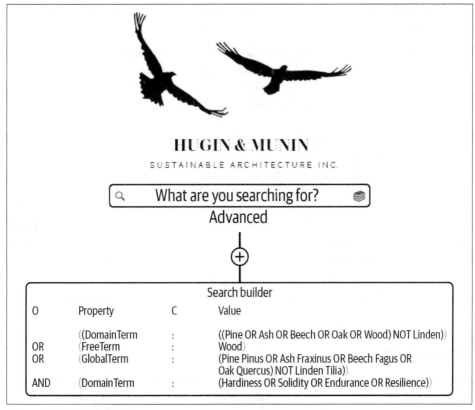

Figure 4-6. *Search builder*

The search builder in Hugin & Munin creates a visually navigable overview of long searches. *O* stands for *operator*, *C* for *condition*. All the parentheses that are gray are optional; they become active if the end user clicks them. This way of cutting up the complex search makes it easier to keep an overview of what the search does, so that the semantics especially are easy to keep an eye on.

 Search builders like the one in Figure 4-6 are standard components in reference databases such as PubMed (*https://oreil.ly/I5scP*). Many data catalogs, such as data.world (*https://oreil.ly/0dmOm*), also have a search builder.

This type of search is also called block search (*https://oreil.ly/1wdUQ*) in LIS. It's practiced as a method to obtain large sets of search results for complex searches. Normally, this kind of search has several phases, where words are added, others removed, in a series of adjustments that make the searcher capable of translating what data is needed to the language and structure of the data catalog, based on analysis of the hits retrieved from the previous steps in the search.

Moreover, this is a kind of search that makes use of how your data catalog glossaries are applied. The higher the specificity—that is, the more the terms from the glossaries are actually applied on the assets in the data catalog (using the exhaustivity of the glossaries), the more your recall mechanism will work.

 Remember Zipf's law from Chapter 3? If you only rely on crawled metadata, your chance of success with block search is low. You need glossary terms applied by humans, not machines, to make your assets distinguishable from each other.

Block search is difficult to build, but it is very important to master. In legal, compliance, and complex searches for innovation use cases, block search is the kind of search that will make or break a positive outcome for your company.

And sometimes you have to do a complex search that is not really a well-defined topic with glossary terms assigned to it, but a more haphazard accumulation of things that someone happens to want to know more about.

Statement Search

Most complex combinatorial searches are *statement searches*: an assorted blend of people, systems, domains, and everything else you can build searches from. These kinds of searches are necessary to make in many disparate situations, ranging from managing the data catalog, to gathering data for a project, to ensuring that assets associated with a given steward who is changing position are passed on to a new steward (for this latter use case, check out Chapter 7 on lifecycles).

Figure 4-7 shows an example of a search performed by the Hugin & Munin data discovery team. They want to find out how many Tableau reports do not have an asset owner in Legal, Finance, or IT.

This search returns all Tableau reports from those departments that have been created after January 1, 2022, that do not have an owner.

The data discovery team will use this search result to reach out to the data stewards for the assets to ask that an owner of the asset be added.

Figure 4-7. Statement search

Browsing Patterns

Browsing patterns are in fact search patterns, but they usually don't require the end user to phrase search statements (except for glossary lookups). Instead, browsing works by clicking back and forth in either lists of glossary terms, lineage, or graphs. Think of browsing as a phase between other types of search that makes users discover and learn the language and domains of their company. It will allow them to search with more savvy if they can browse the data landscape.

Glossary Browsing

Sometimes, you may just want to explore a topic to better understand a domain. You have many options, but one of the ways is to browse glossaries.

An example from Hugin & Munin is a new employee wanting to better understand how paint is used as the surface treatment for wooden houses. The user types "paint" in the dedicated glossary search bar, as seen in Figure 4-8.

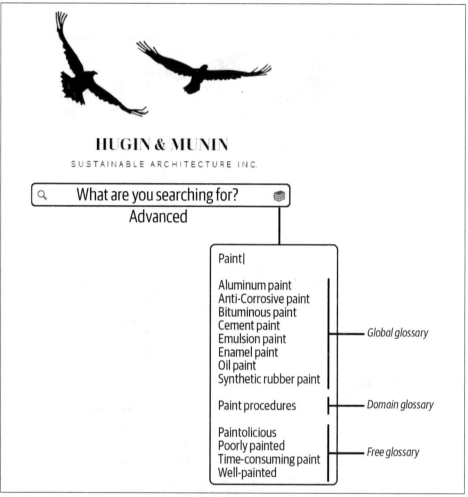

Figure 4-8. Glossary browsing after paint

Here, the difference between the different glossaries stands out clearly: the global glossary is made up of highly controlled terms that apply across the company, the domain glossary refers to a single domain, and the free glossary just adds whatever people like. Clicking deeper into the glossaries reveals the level of organization in them, as depicted in Figure 2-11.

Domain Browsing

Domain browsing is when you go through the capabilities or processes in your company. These kinds of browsings are often driven by lack of context—they allow you to get ideas of where potentially relevant assets could be located. For example, maybe someone is working on a project regarding customer profiles and they want to know if it falls under the purview of Customer Information Management or Customer Preference Management. This might tell them who they need to speak to regarding issues.

They can also just be driven by sheer curiosity—and that kind of browsing is never a waste of time, as it allows you to better understand the data landscape of your company. If you want to see how domain browsing looks, go back to Figure 3-7.

Lineage Browsing

Sometimes, you might want to know where a given asset stems from (upstream), or where it has traveled to (downstream). Browsing upstream in lineage enables you to find out why a given data analytics report is broken. Lineage browsing also allows you to test what the consequences would be downstream of changes in a given asset upstream, if you were to make a change. You could also be browsing lineage to discover potential improvements to existing data processing flows or to discover unused assets in the environment (like a table with flows going in but no flows going out). Or you can search for lineage that has changed (or not changed) in time spans to identify old data pipelines.

A DPO can also document how sensitive data is processed downstream. I show such examples of applied lineage search in Chapter 5.

Remember that lineage functionality will vary from vendor to vendor and that, accordingly, your applied search possibilities will vary: remember to assess lineage functionality in your vendor selection, if this criterion is important to you. This assessment is complex, and it requires substantial time to find the ups and downs of a given lineage functionality. You can, for example, expand lineage to include lineage from the past of a given asset, choose lineage functionality that enriches data lineage with additional metadata to track how high-quality data assets travel, and so on.

Graph Browsing

The ultimate way of browsing your data is by visually exploring your knowledge graph—if your data catalog is built on a knowledge graph, as discussed in Chapters 1 and 2. The knowledge graph links all parts of your data catalog beautifully together. It's the manifestation of all the actual nodes in your metamodel. It's the ideal way to maximize serendipity in your search, as you can click your way around everything in the catalog and discover new connections.

Graphs are excellent at providing overviews of social networks. Graphs are used as such in these two sectors, for example:

- Law enforcement, military, and intelligence services
- Universities and academia in general

For *police, military, and intelligence services,* networks of people and the things they use and have (such as phones, weapons, documents) visually laid out in a graph is an absolute must. In police investigations, graphs can map criminal organizations like Mafia families or gangs and help solve the crimes these organizations commit by displaying how people—and networks of people—are linked. Military strategies and tactics on the battlefield are nowadays powered by graphs; they are part of active warfare to map and defeat the enemy. For intelligence services, graphs generate overviews of networks of extremists under surveillance, such as political or religious extremists. The graph overview helps intelligence agencies to infiltrate and dissolve these networks before they act. Graph solutions for these kinds of organizations are provided by IBM (*https://oreil.ly/k8mlF*) and Palantir (*https://oreil.ly/_4yhh*), for example.

For *universities and academia in general,* graphs are used to map and visualize networks of researchers or research topics. These are bibliometric maps (*https://oreil.ly/M_sd2*) (sometimes also called *clusters* and *networks*). A beautiful example is this bibliometric cluster of mental health research (*https://oreil.ly/KmQ0l*). Bibliometric maps are used to evaluate the performance of research activities in universities, and also in industrial predictions, since patent clusters indicate what kind of products specific industries are planning to launch.

> The examples are included to explain the value of browsing in graphs—and also potentially in data catalogs, where this feature is still in its infancy.

Let's look at an example. In Figure 4-9, a PR manager in the communications department in Hugin & Munin searches for promotion data; some of the search results seem skewed, but it is hard to tell why. The PR manager then searches for "promotion" one more time. The top hit is a dataset with promotion planning details, and the PR manager opens that hit as a graph. The graph visualizes all the terms, processes, and data sources that relate to *promotion.* Suddenly, the PR manager understands why the results are skewed. Someone has added promotion as a free glossary term not to depict communication but to depict career advancement. That term is followed by an exclamation mark (!) because the data catalog automatically detects that it is a duplicate to the domain glossary term, which defines PR activities. Therefore, assets tagged with the free glossary term should be filtered out of the search. With this knowledge, the PR manager can better shape the search to reflect what they are searching for.

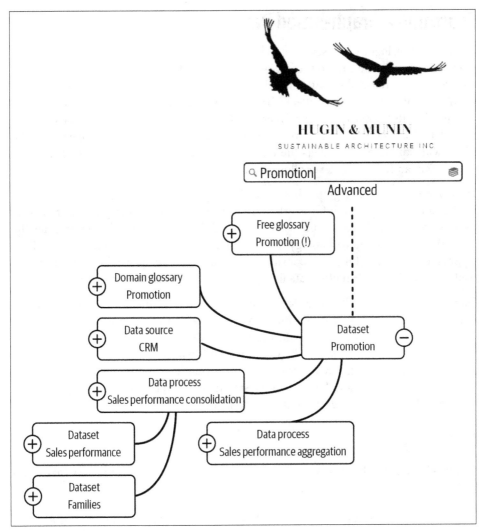

Figure 4-9. Graph browsing

As you have just read, search is a process. In many cases, it will be a series of searches that increase, decrease, and refocus search results, until the search finally matches the information needed.

Searching a Graph-Based Data Catalog

As depicted in Figure 3-4, search can be divided into a spectrum. It goes from easy executable simple searches to more-complex advanced searches. In the latter case, the end user has to remember both the syntax of the IRQL and assess if the semantics of the query statement actually reflect what is being searched for. This is demanding, but useful. The IRQL that the user searches with has been designed by the data catalog provider—I consider DCQL as the minimum acceptable IRQL. It is likely that the IRQL will expand over time, as the technology evolves with the feedback from customers. But an IRQL will never allow you to search for *everything*.

However, for knowledge graph–based data catalogs, it is possible to push search even further and actually search for everything in the data catalog. It requires search skills beyond the IRQL of the specific catalog: instead, here you would have to master the DQL that matches the technology of the catalog in question, for example, SPARQL, Cypher, or Gremlin. Take into consideration that data lineage can be graph-based as well and that, if so, this makes data lineage searchable in a similar fashion.

Searching with a DQL inside a data catalog requires a technical skill set that not all data catalog use cases rely upon. But if you truly want to organize your data just as you like, and search it however you want, then this is what it takes. Think of it like this: an IRQL is always designed by the provider; it will contain some of the elements that are useful to search for, and leave others out. But the graph DQL lets you search for everything you want because it is set up to search for everything that the metamodel contains, however it has been defined.

Summary

In this chapter you have become familiar with how to apply search. Key takeaways include:

- When searching for data, you need to apply the mindset of a librarian, not a data scientist. Searching for data is a discipline that relies on search mechanics, but it also takes experience and understanding your company's data and language.

- *Basic simple search* is the way of searching that most end users will apply. A well-structured data catalog will deliver precise simple search, especially if it's based on a knowledge graph. But expect a lot of mess deeper down in the search results also.

- *Detailed simple search* requires you to know the syntax of the IRQL in your data catalog. So it takes a little time to write, or just experience, but you get super-precise hits in return.

- *Flexible simple search* also depends on understanding IRQL, but it opens up the search to give more results, increasing your recall and decreasing your precision, while at the same time still being a better way to target a well-defined topic than *basic simple search*.
- *Range search* is searching in intervals, e.g., a time span. This kind of search will result in high precision and low recall.
- *Block search* is a structured way to search for a complex topic using IRQL. It works best if your glossaries are exhaustive and used with great specificity.
- *Statement search* is a way to search for a complex topic; it simply puts a lot of things together in a search. It's not unstructured, but it's haphazard.
- *Glossary browsing* is searching in which you go exploring to get informed and enlightened about business terminology.
- *Domain browsing, lineage browsing,* and *graph browsing* are ways of searching vertically, horizontally, and relationally, respectively, by clicking through the data landscape.

In the next chapter, we will look at how engaging with stakeholders makes all the difference when implementing the data catalog. If everyone understands the value of the data catalog and uses it properly, implementation will go very smoothly. But that is not always the case, and the next chapter goes through how to unite stakeholders for a well-developed data catalog.

Democratizing Data with a Data Catalog

The second part of this book is about a fortunate development in the global data community that is supported by technology: data democratization. Data democratization is about how more and more employees in companies are able to discover, access, and manage data, independently, without needing the assistance of a small, central data team. A data catalog contributes to this development by covering three major aspects of data democratization: how to *discover, access,* and *manage* data, which I will cover in this section.

In Chapter 5, "Discover Data: Empower End Users and Engage Stakeholders", you will take a look at the idea of the data catalog as a social network and how the main stakeholders of a data catalog can benefit from it by discovering data and better fulfilling their tasks.

Then, Chapter 6, "Access Data: The Keys to Successful Implementation", goes into the technical discussions of how you can provide access to data. Smooth access to data is a key parameter for a successful data catalog implementation.

Finally, in Chapter 7, "Manage Data: Improve Lifecycle Management", you will be introduced to the lifecycles of data. These lifecycles can be very difficult to manage, but the data catalog is the key to the solution, leading to better data management altogether.

CHAPTER 5

Discover Data: Empower End Users and Engage Stakeholders

The more users a data catalog has, and the more these users can do independently of the central discovery team, the more quality the data catalog will provide. As such, users must be engaged with the data catalog in a way that makes them connect as a social network.

Activating the metadata in the data catalog in the tools where employees carry out daily tasks is one way to empower end users. Another important aspect is to engage the main stakeholders in the leadership of your organization. If they understand the value of a data catalog, they are likely to drive engagement and participation with their constituents.

A Data Catalog Is a Social Network

The success of your data catalog depends on user adoption. A data catalog is a collaborative tool. It is successful only if many people use it actively and in a federated way. Every employee must be offered the opportunity to add data to the catalog, search, comment, request, share, and use data with everyone else, perhaps with collaboration from a colleague, maybe two, but ideally not with support from the central data discovery team. If this level of cooperation is not reached in the data catalog, it will not become effective.

> You want the usage of a data catalog to be as federated as possible, with each domain being able to expose, provide, and consume data as independently as possible of the data discovery team.

If employees can't learn from their closest colleagues in using the data catalog, then they will line up to wait for help from the central data discovery team, to help organize all data, search for data, and help provide access to data. That will slow the offerings of the data catalog and ultimately become its quiet assassin: the data catalog will not prove useful since it relies on many users to be able to perform the tasks inside it before it provides value.

Imagine that you are an end user who has just discovered an interesting data asset. Say you request access to that asset. Either the owner of the asset can approve that directly, or your request must pass through an intermediary such as, for example, the data discovery team, in order for you to get access to the asset. If the latter is the case, you lose time as the request becomes added to a workload in the data discovery team and complexity arises because the request needs to be explained to that team as well.

Figure 5-1 displays weak and strong networks of employees interacting in a data catalog. The weak network is dependent on a few key persons who connect everyone in the network, whereas the strong network connects everyone in the network with many other people directly.

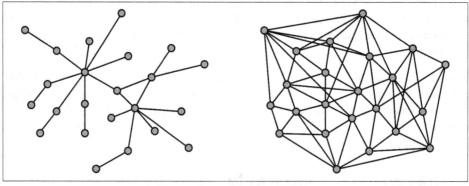

Figure 5-1. Weak network (left) and strong network (right)

The more users who are directly connected in regard to all the tasks that can be performed in the data catalog, the stronger your data catalog is. Now, if we extrapolate that situation to all users of the catalog, then a clear pattern emerges. Many people in the network is not necessarily a good thing; it depends on how they are connected. If your data catalog has many end users who are not directly connected, that is, not capable of searching, understanding, and sharing data directly with each other, then your network is big and weak. If, on the other hand, your data catalog does not have many end users, but those end users are well connected, then your data catalog is powerful. And that's how you must grow it, adding more and more domains that are strong and independent, capable of performing all the tasks in the catalog. The more people who can interact in all sorts of ways directly, the more effective your data catalog is.

The key to a strong network is a capability on the rise—namely, that of activating your metadata.

Active Metadata

I have argued that data catalogs are tools that must organize data so that it can be searched for, smoothly and effectively, in as many ways as possible. Data catalogs fail if they just map a data landscape but nobody explores that landscape. Therefore, metadata must be activated. Accordingly, a new term has emerged, *active metadata*, and it is a mandatory element in future data catalogs.

Active metadata is about getting beyond the point of just mapping data. The true success of a data catalog is when it is searched intensely by the entire company. Active metadata takes this vision to the next level. Gartner has specified four characteristics of active metadata:[1]

- Always on
- Intelligent
- Action-oriented
- Open by default

Specifically for data catalogs, this means:

Always on
> The data catalog should contain a fresh representation of the data landscape—its crawlers run repeatedly or streaming is not turned off.

Intelligent
> The description of data is constantly improved by natural language processing and machine learning, to increase potentially relevant hits when searching.

Action-oriented
> Notifications and recommendations should be pushed to end users, so that they are nudged to discover even more data.

Open by default
> This is a true game changer. The data catalog can be considered an octopus, spreading its tentacles in every direction to display all the data it encounters on its way. But with API-based approaches, it is also possible to mirror the data catalog back into every data tool where it would be of relevance to search for the data within the data catalog, such as a BI tool.

---

1 Gartner 2021: Market Guide for Active Metadata Management (*https://oreil.ly/a3qyj*).

Active metadata, therefore, is an approach that makes use of data catalogs as one of its most vital elements, but it exceeds the data catalog itself and spreads the potential of data into all other data-consuming applications. You would have the search bar from the data catalog in your BI tool, in your CMDB, and so on—you wouldn't need to move into the catalog itself to search for data.

Employees are reluctant to leave their daily tools to log in to the catalog and do something there, and active metadata is a recognition of that. It does not change the importance of proper search; it changes the way this search capability (including other capabilities described in previous chapters) can be made available to all potential users of the data catalog.

Prukalpa Sankar, cofounder of the Atlan data catalog that specializes in active metadata capabilities, has put forward several use cases for active metadata,[2] which are also detailed on Atlan's website (*https://oreil.ly/l4Zpj*). One of their use cases is impacting downstream users of data via Slack or Jira when the data they consume changes (*https://oreil.ly/QXZQm*). Several tech providers offer active metadata capabilities, like MANTA and illumex (*https://oreil.ly/HJ-8K*).

> Later in this chapter, I discuss the *operational backbone* and the *data platform* in companies. Active metadata can play a role in both. Active metadata can heavily impact and improve a company data platform because it can push data toward the use cases where the value is highest. For the operational backbone, active metadata can, for example, push notifications of PII being discovered in a newly crawled data source.

Certain vendors promote their technology as being an active metadata platform. At a closer look, these technologies offer many of the same capabilities as technologies marketed as data catalogs. Therefore, I advise you to identify the capabilities delivered by the technologies you are considering for your company more than the type of technology these vendors categorize themselves as. There is no fine line between data catalogs and active metadata management platforms. Instead of asking yourself what category of technology you want, ask yourself what capabilities you want.

At a minimum, data catalog users must consist of data analysts and scientists who will be using the catalog to search for data and data engineers and stewards who are setting up the catalog and populating it. Ideally, they should come from domains across the business. But furthermore, as metadata is the key to unlocking a true data-driven culture in organizations, we must find ways into the minds and hearts of the everyday

---

2 Prukalpa Sankar, "What Is Active Metadata, and Why Does It Matter?" (*https://oreil.ly/SERhz*) Towards Data Science (medium.com), May 2022.

end users who use data rarely, search in less complex ways, and have simple information needs. That is why active metadata is so critical to have, to offer the capabilities of the data catalog in the tool that the everyday end users are already using, not the data catalog itself. That said, on top of an active metadata capability is the future potential of the company search engine, which I discuss in Chapter 8. It will be a search capability so strong, it will automatically draw all users toward it.

 In Chapter 8 of this book, I foresee a "turn." Let's consider data catalogs as closed capabilities that open with active metadata. The turn I suggest in Chapter 8 is that data catalogs will become company search engines, and as such, their search capability will be so strong that they will naturally attract more users to search and work from inside them.

Now, let's discuss the most important users of the data catalog.

Ensure Stakeholder Engagement

A robust data catalog with many empowered users and connected assets needs the support of its stakeholders. This section describes how to gain stakeholder engagement. You need to get engagement from:

- Data governance leaders
- Data analytics leaders
- Domain leaders

Whether you're part of the team implementing the data catalog or part of leadership, advocate for open communication and education. In this section, I'll explain the perspectives of these stakeholders and show you how a data catalog aligns with their priorities. I'll also give you tips on how to communicate the benefits of a data catalog to these leaders.

If you're one of these stakeholders, great! Read on and learn how you fit into the bigger picture of a data catalog social network.

Engage Data Governance Leaders

The data governance leaders are typically the data protection officer (DPO) and chief information security officer (CISO).

The DPO protects personal data from being exploited by your company. The DPO does this by ensuring that your company complies with regulations such as the European Union General Data Protection Regulation (GDPR) or California Privacy Rights Act (CPRA) and similar. To do so, the DPO needs to identify and ensure the correct processing of personal *sensitive* data in the company. This data cannot be processed in any other way than what has been consented to by the person in scope.

The CISO works on protecting your company's data from cyberattacks and industrial espionage—hostile intentions from the world outside. The CISO works on a risk-based approach as defined in documentation such as *ISO/IEC 27000* series. Key to the CISO role is therefore to identify and correctly secure *confidential* data, and the less hassle the CISO has in doing so, the more complex risk measures can be addressed.

Figure 5-2 illustrates that the DPO and the CISO in fact do the same thing, with opposite purposes. The DPO protects the world from the company, and the CISO protects the company from the world.

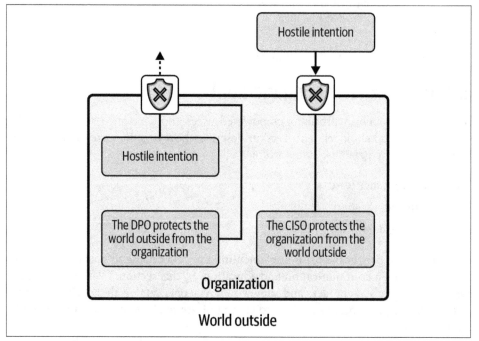

Figure 5-2. The DPO and CISO in the organization do the same thing with opposite purposes

 Because the DPO and CISO do the same thing, albeit with opposite purposes, their methodology is very similar. Accordingly, *ISO/IEC 27700* series further coordinate the formalized procedures for DPOs and CISOs into one set of standards.

Because the DPO and the CISO do the same thing, they both have maps of what they try to protect: all the data in the company. The maps might not be complete because they are manually updated. The CISO does this in an information security management system (ISMS), and the DPO does this in a privacy information management system (PIMS).

The data catalog allows the data governance leaders to join forces, save time, and excel by supporting the implementation of the data catalog. With a data catalog, DPOs and CISOs do not need to map all the data in the company in their PIMS and ISMS. They can focus on helping the company reach the perfect classification of sensitivity and confidentiality, directly on data—and not in policies, SOPs, and guidelines.

As you will see in the following, thanks to advanced data lineage capabilities, they are able to map, understand, and document details of data processing to get even more visibility in how sensitive data moves in the company and thus better comply with numerous existing privacy regulations.

Some PIMSs and ISMSs are sold with a data catalog component, and some data catalogs are sold as being capable of performing the tasks inside PIMSs and ISMSs. But you should avoid such a blend; these solutions are not the same. Both the PIMS and the ISMS are process tools based on ISO's management cycle: Plan, Do, Check, Act (PDCA). Accordingly, they ensure a continuous minimization of risks associated with information security and data protection. A data catalog is not such a tool.

The data catalog also delivers a unique data governance capability to the DPO and CISO: classification of sensitivity and confidentiality labels directly on data.

As mentioned, DPOs and CISOs work with policies, SOPs, and guidelines that explain how sensitive and confidential data can be, conceptually. It's up to each employee to interpret those policies and decide if a given asset falls into one or the other categories of sensitivity and confidentiality. With the data catalog, individual interpretation is no longer necessary. Data protection policies and information security policies can be translated into labels of sensitivity and confidentiality directly on the assets. This is a big win! Employees will know what data is sensitive and what is confidential just by looking at it.

When working with the DPO and CISO, be sure to involve them with the implementation of the data catalog by asking for their input. As an example, ask them to assess a dataset that is sensitive, and let them browse that dataset in lineage to see how analytics is performed on it downstream. They can evaluate if that usage is in accordance with the consent the individuals in the dataset have given. Take their input and incorporate it into the implementation of the data. Show them a visualization of downstream data lineage, such as the one for Hugin & Munin as shown in Figure 5-3. Not only will this exercise give you input to make the data catalog better aligned with data governance needs, but it will help the CISO and DPO realize that they can govern all the data in the company with the support of the data catalog.

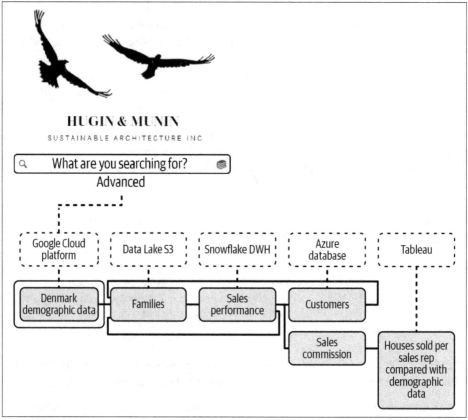

Figure 5-3. Applied search example: lineage downstream to demonstrate the usage of sensitive data

Specifically for the DPO, keep in mind that this role has a lot of responsibilities related to existing data privacy regulations such as GDPR, California Consumer Privacy Act (CCPA)/CPRA, and others. A big part of those regulations is understanding what PII data a company has, but also how it is being processed. That's why it will be so effective to show a DPO data lineage.

GDPR contains a *record of processing activities* (RoPA), and it's difficult and time-consuming to document manually. And furthermore, it's not exact when only done manually. Data lineage not only gives insights about relationships between data assets but also details how they are processed downstream. This significantly simplifies the RoPA process, and it will significantly help with engaging your DPO.

Engage Data Analytics Leaders

Your organization probably has a multitude of data analytics leaders. They will work with machine learning, natural language processing, business intelligence (BI), artificial intelligence, and other types of data analytics. The data analytics roles vary; they are not formalized as are data governance roles. Instead, data analytics roles depend on the strategic priorities of your company.

Regardless of their job titles, data analytics stakeholders need an overview of what data the organization has, which is exactly what a data catalog can provide. The more overview they get, the more value they can deliver. Data analytics leaders are very likely to make practical use of the data catalog themselves.

Let's look at a typical use case. A *head of BI* is responsible for a team that maintains a platform to create BI reports—all parts of the company use that platform to create all kinds of reports. Let's say that the BI team has a problem: inside the BI platform, all datasets are confidential and cannot be shared with the entire organization. Users can only see what they are allowed to, so they create their own reports, thus creating duplicates and unnecessary work. One solution is to use a data catalog so the content of the BI platform can be exposed with all reports at a metadata level, as we discussed in Chapter 1. This accelerates data analytics in a very tangible way. All employees can now see what reports exist in total in the company. They no longer need to reinvent the wheel and can now devote their time to more useful projects.

 Analytical competition can be exciting. Suggest a friendly competition between your data analytics leaders and ask them to see who can expose their analytical reports and dashboards the fastest in the data catalog. The benefits to this are twofold. Not only will your data analytics leaders get to test their skills and take pride in showing their work, but it will highlight the usefulness of the data catalog for innovation.

Data catalogs are also useful for data analytics leaders. They can apply search to enhance innovation services to the business. For example, the head of BI and similar functions is interested in lineage upstream because reporting sometimes breaks. When this happens, the numbers suddenly don't make sense, even though they used to. They stop making sense because of reconfiguration of data in the data sources upstream. This is where a data catalog comes in. Figure 5-4 shows how it is to search a report in the data catalog, find it, and then browse upstream in its lineage to see where the data in the report is coming from and subsequently how to fix it.

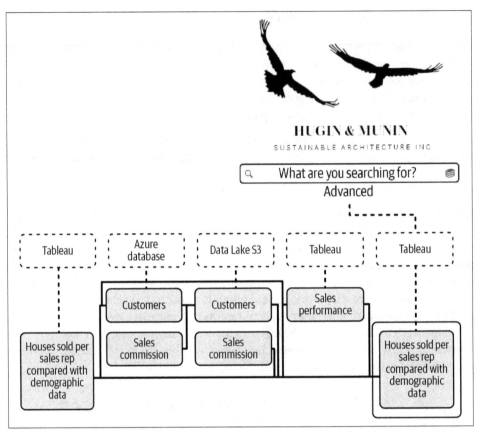

Figure 5-4. Applied search example: lineage upstream to fix broken values in a Tableau report

This may launch additional activities, because once they identify the root cause and they know where the issue is, they must also ask a follow-up question: "Which other reports and analytical assets—and/or any other data assets in my company—were impacted by the same issue?" Those assets, of course, also need to be fixed.

In general, data lineage creates trust in data. Data analytics teams feel more comfortable when knowing the data source upstream in lineage. There is less doubt about the trustworthiness of data.

With data lineage, it is not only possible to trace the root cause of broken data. You can also apply data lineage in a preventive way, in the sense that data source owners can see what would be the consequences of changes in their systems downstream.

Engage Domain Leaders

Domain leaders are the leaders in line of business who take care of the value chain of the company. They are often busy with daily operations and do not have the capacity to take on additional tasks. To promote domain leader engagement, focus on showing them how to use the data catalog to fulfill their data needs.[3] Remember that the active metadata approach suggests that they stay inside their primary analytics tool, from which they can use the data catalog search capabilities.

Let's consider the finance department, for example. Finance needs to know the overall economic performance of the company. It furthermore needs to know the performance of each product the company has on the market and so on in order to do the annual accounts. Therefore, finance relies on the sales department to report that data. The more and the deeper the data from sales is, the more finance can do with it, beyond the mandatory accounting required by the authorities. If finance can get rich, deep data from sales, it can do detailed economic forecasting and other predictive analytics that can help executive management make strategic decisions.

You can explain this and show applied search to finance. Prepare for that in advance by making a couple of small, fictive reports with intricate sales data analytics. Then, pull those reports to a test environment in the data catalog. Finally, show to finance that they can search and find such reports, like in Figure 5-5. Let the employees in finance really imagine what it's like to easily search the data that could make them work smarter and deliver more strategic input to their peers and executive management.

---

3 You can find many overviews of typical information needs in companies in G. G. Chowdhury, *Introduction to Modern Information Retrieval* (New York: Neal-Schuman Publishers, 2010), 230–32.

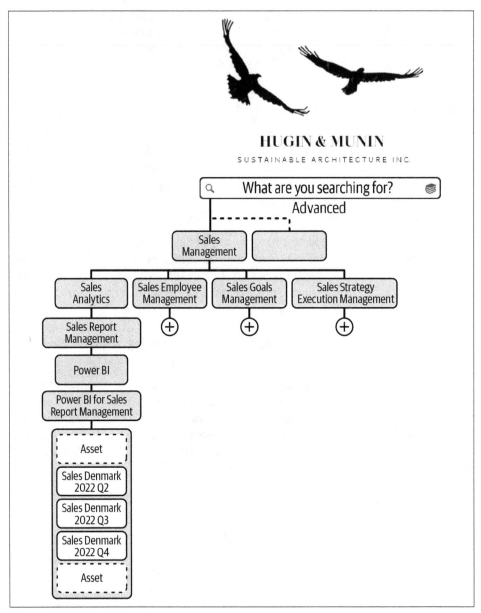

Figure 5-5. Sales reporting displayed for finance

Do this demonstration with every department in the company. Be sure to customize each demonstration with the needs of each particular department so it is immediately relatable. By showcasing how the data catalog helps them do their jobs better, you're framing the data catalog as something that is meant to help them, rather than a burden. This kind of positive interaction will encourage engagement with the data catalog.

Finally, let's look at how all these leaders are in fact connected.

Seeing All Data Through One Lens

All leaders—data governance leaders, data analytics leaders, and domain leaders—work with data, and they see data through their own distinct lens. A DPO will ask: "How sensitive is this data?" A CISO will ask: "How confidential is this data?" A data analytics leader will ask: "What insights can I get from this data?" And the domain leader will ask: "What part of the value chain does this data support?" In the previous section, we discussed all this separately. In this section, you will see that all these ways of looking at data are in fact intricately connected.

All companies use data in their daily activities, but there is a fundamental distinction to take into account. Data can be used in two places, on the operational backbone and the data platform, which we will discuss now.

The Operational Backbone and the Data Platform

The *operational backbone* consists of the IT solutions that carry out the processes in the value chain of the company. IT in this context creates more robust and increased production, but the processes and the products remain the same. The operational backbone relies on *process integration*: integrations between systems that orchestrate a part of the value chain—processes. This requires high data quality, even Master Data Management (MDM)—as bad data can break the value chain. Basically, the operational backbone runs the business, as stated by Ross et al. in *Designed for Digital*:

> An operational backbone provides a tightly integrated, bulletproof production environment ensuring the reliability and security of business processes.[4]

As an example, consider an integration between an enterprise resource planning (ERP) system and the product information management (PIM) system. The ERP is highly reliant on the PIM to provide precise data on all the products that the ERP system itself contains data about: what products are in which warehouses, what products have been shipped to which clients, etc. This is the operational backbone at work; data is used to carry out processes in the company.

A *data platform* consists of several components and applications that allow you to store, discover, query, and visualize data. This data has become independent of the operational backbone. Again, quoting from *Designed for Digital*:

---

4 Jeanne W. Ross et al., *Designed for Digital: How to Architect Your Business for Sustained Success* (Cambridge, MA: The MIT Press, 2019), chap. 4, p. 58.

A digital platform [I use the term *data platform*] is a *repository of business, data and infrastructure components used to rapidly configure digital offerings.* What's so special about a digital platform? Reusable digital components. ... To succeed digitally, companies must define data, business, and infrastructure components and design them for reuse.[5]

In contrast to the operational backbone, the data platform does not support existing processes. Instead, it exposes data and makes it consumable and reusable.[6] It's the unlocking of data that is becoming the do-or-die of companies in the 2020s, and it requires a methodology, such as *data mesh* or *data management at scale*, as cited throughout this book.

You can see an illustration of the operational backbone and the data platform in Figure 5-6. Do note that both the backbone and the platform must be exposed in a data catalog to be fully performing, discoverable, and governed.

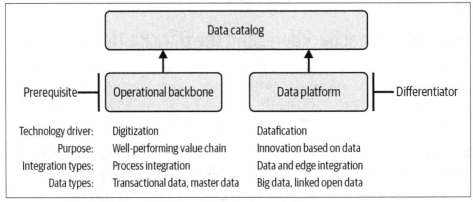

Figure 5-6. The operational backbone and the data platform

The companies that offer the best data platform on top of a well-performing operational backbone win the market. These companies do not just offer the same products, produced with ever-increasing efficiency as a result of *digitization* of their value chain. Instead, they continuously modify, refine, and reinvent their products based on data. Such companies capture, analyze, and understand their customers based on, e.g., data that the customers produce through their behavior. This again is a consequence of *datafication*. Datafication conceptualizes that more and more human

---

5 Ibid., 59.

6 I do not discuss business and infrastructure components in detail. *Infrastructure* components are, e.g., identity and access management (IAM) components. *Business* components is a synonym for data and analytics tools, such as BI tools.

behavior generates data, as it is increasingly performed with or monitored by digital tools such as smartphones.[7]

This is where your data governance leaders come into play, because datafication leads to *dataveillance*. Dataveillance is surveillance performed on the basis of data—in this case, on the data platform. Dataveillance is filtering, curating, and organizing datafied human activity. Data platforms must perform dataveillance on datafied activity; if they do not, they can't operate. This is why data governance ensures customer acceptance of the collection of their personal data and defines how it can be processed. But the operational backbone also holds both sensitive and confidential data. So also here lies a task that is very important for the DPO to execute.

The purpose of implementing a data catalog is to support this. Both data from the operational backbone and from the data platform must be exposed in the data catalog. When all this data is represented at the metadata level in the data catalog, then the efficiency of the company increases remarkably. A complete overview of the data landscape in the data catalog offers an optimized operational backbone and a rich data platform, while having both the backbone and the platform firmly governed.

 For domain leaders, data is mostly used to perform and smoothen the operational backbone. Running operational data is hard, requiring precision and most of the domain leader's time. Domain leaders also use some analytical data, but mostly operational data. Data analytics leaders use some operational data, but only for analytical purposes—they are unattached to the operational backbone. Therefore, data analytics leaders depend more on a data platform.

Compare this with the reality of the operational backbone defining its own metadata and understanding its data in its own way, both completely different from the data platform, with a governance on top that tries to manage this.

Summary

In this chapter, you learned how to gain stakeholder engagement and strengthen the social and data connections of a data catalog. Key takeaways include:

- A data catalog is a social network; the persons in it can be connected in weak and strong ways. In order for the data catalog to be a success, many people must be strongly connected and be able to autonomously expose, search, request, and share data.

---

7 For the concepts "datafication" and "dataveillance," see Rob Kitchin, *The Data Revolution: A Critical Analysis of Big Data, Open Data and Data Infrastructures* (London: Sage, 2022).

- Data catalogs must activate metadata so that a data catalog is not just a dead repository of data but a machine that pushes relevant data in contexts where it can provide value and increased results.

- Data governance leaders are engaged by the fact that they can apply sensitivity and confidentiality classification directly on data. They are furthermore motivated by the fact that they can join forces in mapping the IT landscape and concentrate on more strategic priorities.

- Data analytics leaders are engaged naturally, but an extra selling point is data lineage, which allows these leaders to understand changes upstream or the causes of broken reporting.

- Domain leaders are engaged by the potential of seeing data from other business units that they are in need of in their daily tasks.

- All leaders are in fact connected. They work with data for different purposes, either on the operational backbone or on the data platform. But the data they work with is the same, and they need to align on how to describe it and manage it in a data catalog.

In the next chapter, we'll go through what it takes to implement a data catalog from the very beginning.

CHAPTER 6

Access Data: The Keys to Successful Implementation

This is not a chapter on the *actual* implementation of data catalogs, but a chapter on the most important decisions you must take *before* you implement a data catalog.

I'll show you what to consider when choosing a data catalog, in what ways you can create access to the data you find in the data catalog, and finally, the questions domain owners and asset stewards must ask themselves to describe their domain and its assets.

First, let's look at the selection criteria for a data catalog.

Choosing a Data Catalog

Most data catalogs specialize in one or more of the different capabilities I list in the following, such as data lineage or sharing agreements, how it is possible to organize data, or how they adapt to a specific tech stack. No data catalog out there does everything perfectly (such as the fictitious data catalog used by the equally fictitious Hugin & Munin company), though there are many that do certain things very well. Furthermore, you may prefer how one data catalog does something over another. The key is to know what you need from a data catalog.

Vendor Analysis

The first step to figuring out which data catalog is right for your organization is to determine what you need from a data catalog. You might want a data catalog that specializes in one or more capabilities, and so the following overview is created to help you perform your vendor analysis.

Take a look at Chapter 8. In that chapter, you will find advice on how data catalogs will evolve. This might affect your choice in the present, as some future trends can be taken into consideration as well when selecting a data catalog.

Generally, this book is written from a tech-agnostic, enterprise architecture perspective because that is what will help you the most for the longest period of time when working with data catalogs. When choosing your data catalog, you'll want to first consider the enterprise architecture specified capabilities because they are more permanent than the technology that executes it:

- Data lineage
- Data sharing
- On premises
- Custom build
- Single cloud provider
- One platform
- Data intelligence
- Data governance
- Knowledge graph–powered data catalogs
- Data observability
- Catalog of catalogs

Before I explain what you need to consider for each capability, bear in mind that the list is technology-specific. This is to provide you with more context of the landscape of data catalog vendors as of 2022–23. Although the capabilities discussed in the list will remain relevant for a long period of time, the vendors mentioned may change their name, focus, or performance. As with anything in IT, capabilities are stable—the specific technology changes and evolves constantly. Check the vendor websites for up-to-date information.

Some Key Vendors

Data lineage is a standard feature in many data catalogs, but certain vendors specialize in deep, very complex data lineage for large and diverse IT landscapes. Data lineage is a vital component for automating the documentation of how data is processed in your company and enabling enterprise-wide search to understand dependencies upstream and downstream between assets.

As an alternative to manually built Visio diagrams and PowerPoint slides, data lineage is an always up-to-date and accurate map of how data actually moves—it's empirically based, whereas Visio diagrams and the like will always hold an element of uncertainty and decrease in freshness from the moment they are created, contrary to data lineage, which is updated on an ongoing basis. As discussed in Chapter 5, in the data lineage field, companies such as Octopai (*https://oreil.ly/KpX6E*) and MANTA (*https://oreil.ly/ps4fi*) are key players.

Data sharing is an emerging capability as more than a simple "request" button in data catalogs. Data contracts and the quality of the shared data can be measured to indicate to what extent data delivered by the data provider matches the demands from the data consumer. In this discipline, Great Expectations (*https://oreil.ly/7RS5v*) is surfacing as a first mover.

On premises is a heavy, complex focus for many companies successfully running and using business-critical systems and applications developed in the pre-cloud era, or companies that are in need of on-premises data centers, e.g., for manufacturing processes. Certain data catalogs handle on-premises complexity as a dedicated focus, especially Informatica (*https://oreil.ly/-PHoH*) (which also performs in the cloud!).

Custom build is also an option—you can build your own data catalog. But with so many vendors in this space, it's rarely a good choice to follow a build-before-buy enterprise architecture principle. Such an approach needs to be assessed carefully, unless the needed solution is either so simple that a spreadsheet is sufficient or so complex that no vendor can cater to that need. In such a case, consider if a data catalog is really what is needed.

Single cloud provider refers to data catalogs that come out of the box from a cloud provider. Some examples include Purview (*https://oreil.ly/NG2yX*) for Microsoft Azure, Data Catalog for Google Cloud Platform (*https://oreil.ly/h3zLe*), and Glue Data Catalog (*https://oreil.ly/maXF-*) for Amazon Web Services. If your company relies on only one cloud provider, then the data catalog of that specific cloud provider is an obvious choice to consider, because it fits the tech stack it is native to.

One platform is similar to the cloud provider, only it's not a complete cloud provider but a major platform that your company uses. Such platform data catalogs include SAP's catalog (*https://oreil.ly/_G4XV*) and Palantir's data catalog (*https://oreil.ly/_SWkt*). If your company runs on one platform, consider using that platform's data catalog because it fits the tech stack it is native to.

Data intelligence is a strategic use case for data catalogs that require a vast set of components to work. As a concept, *data intelligence* is an umbrella term for using the data catalog in most of the ways described in this book; that is, both for governance and for analytics, as well as, for example, for cloud migration. After all, the main driver for data catalogs is the intelligence they allow for, but for catalogs to focus so broadly, they usually have to have a lot of well-established features that have proven their worth in a certain amount of time. In this space you can find some of the more established data catalogs such as Collibra (*https://oreil.ly/9yJ5j*) and Alation (*https://oreil.ly/55rF9*).

Data governance is a key component delivered by most data catalogs with various levels of depth. As a standout capability, it is not enough to provide access control mechanisms or retention alerts to data assets. A data catalog that focuses on data governance as its primary capability must monitor and mirror the requirements put forward in standards and regulations for data governance, e.g., the ISO 27000 series and GDPR. Such a data catalog might be the right solution if the regulatory/compliance element is the most important for your company (however, watch out and heed the warnings about data governance in Chapter 5). A data catalog that has been built directly on a platform that responds to the requirements in data privacy regulations such as GDPR is found in, e.g., OneTrust (*https://oreil.ly/_CdZ_*).

Knowledge graph–powered data catalogs allow for flexible metamodeling. This type of data catalog allows you to model the universe of knowledge in your company in an ontology, and hence improve search to its maximum capabilities, like search engines on the open web. Zeenea (*https://oreil.ly/NUy0h*) and data.world (*https://oreil.ly/ie9Yq*) are knowledge graph–powered data catalogs.

> Knowledge graph–powered data catalogs are likely to gain increasing influence in the future. They are built on the same technology as the search engines on the web, and they are prone to perform just as well when it comes to effective, simple search. See Chapter 8 and the Afterword for my vision of the data catalog as a company search engine.

Data observability can be performed with a streaming-based approach to data catalogs, which lets users observe data in real time. It's an expensive setup, but also very powerful. This meticulous and instant overview of all changes/updates to data predicts errors and prevents mess. If your company relies heavily on streaming data, you should consider data observability. Keep in mind that data observability requires a data catalog with very strong data lineage capabilities (or integrated with a specialized data lineage solution) to perform at its best (it needs an overview of data). However, a data observability component is not necessarily an integrated part of data catalogs, but an add-on component. A streaming-based, open source data catalog is DataHub (*https://oreil.ly/Vey2F*), with the commercial variant Acryl Data (*https://oreil.ly/yBSgt*). Other players in the data observability space are Acceldata (*https://oreil.ly/ifDQ5*), Anomalo (*https://oreil.ly/NNB59*), Ataccama (*https://oreil.ly/NXRbR*), Bigeye (*https://oreil.ly/L6WZv*), Kensu (*https://oreil.ly/0GmW2*), and Monte Carlo (*https://oreil.ly/n-Q8g*). I discuss data observability more in Chapter 7.

You may also find yourself in a more complex setup with more than one data catalog.

Catalog of Catalogs

Some companies implement a catalog of catalogs—that is, a catalog that sits on top of other catalogs and exposes contents from all of them. The catalog of catalogs is not an ideal pattern—you should strive to implement one data catalog, and one only. Nevertheless, in at least three cases it can be reasonable to consider implementing a catalog of catalogs that can unite:

- Isolated, past implementations of data catalogs
- Hybrids of multicloud and on-premises data catalogs
- Distinct, powerful features from various data catalogs

Let's run through the three cases:

Unite isolated, past implementations of data catalogs
   If your company is decentralized or very decentralized with multiple, independent business units, maybe even globally distributed,[1] then it is possible that several parts of the business have already implemented a data catalog. Those catalogs have distinctively served the part of the business wherein they were implemented. In this case, the catalog of catalogs is merely a synthesis of prior attempts to get an overview of the data landscape in the company.

Unite multicloud and on-premises data catalogs
   It may be that you work in a company that has on-premises data centers combined with a multicloud setup (more than one cloud provider). If that is the case, then you can exploit the advantages of the data catalogs of those cloud providers along with a data catalog specialized in on-premises setups. All those data catalogs should then refer up to a data catalog on top of them all.

Unite distinct, powerful features from various data catalog
   Finally, you may also apply a more bold strategy. Data catalogs have different capabilities. Some specialize in data lineage, others in data sharing, others again apply graph structures that are browsable. Your company can choose to enjoy all the power of those catalogs by implementing them all and making them refer to a catalog of catalogs via APIs.

 To deliver powerful solutions, many data catalog vendors actually partner with each other. This means that, for example, data lineage in one data catalog can be powered by another data catalog vendor, and so on. Examine this during vendor selection.

---

1 Svyatoslav Kotusev, *The Practice of Enterprise Architecture: A Modern Approach to Business and IT Alignment* (Melbourne: SK Publishing, 2021), 311.

How should data found in a data catalog be accessed? This question must have an answer prior to the implementation of a data catalog. That is what we will discuss next.

How to Access Data

There is a difference between search engines for the web and data catalogs. On the web, when you search and find things you want to access, it's just a matter of clicking the link in the search result, which takes you directly to the web page, the source. That's the true beauty of Tim Berners-Lee's original vision of the World Wide Web from the early 1990s: the web is open—everyone can access everything, and everything can be linked together.

In a company, you're just not that lucky—yet. When you search and find things in the data catalog, you click the link, which takes you to a detailed description of the asset you are curious about. But at the metadata level only. To gain access to the actual data, you have to click a button that says "Request," and from that point on, several things can happen. This is the fundamental difference between the open web and the closed IT landscape in a company that relies on data governance policies that define who can access what data.

It's important to have a setup for how data can be accessed once it's found in the data catalog, simply because if interesting data can be accessed only via unstandardized, time-consuming, and complex procedures, then the data catalog will disappoint users and soon lose momentum. Therefore, the question of searching and accessing data needs to be defined prior to the implementation of the data catalog.

The first key is to understand that searching and accessing data is dependent on two roles that each user of the data catalog can have.

Data Providers and Data Consumers

When sharing data directly, there are two roles at play, a data provider and a data consumer. All users who expose their data at a metadata level in a data catalog are to be considered *data providers*: they can provide certain data upon request. Also, every user of the data catalog can search and find metadata inside the data catalog. As you can see in Figure 6-1, at the point when a user searches and finds the data they want to look at, they push a "request" button on the data asset in the catalog. That makes this particular user a *data consumer*.

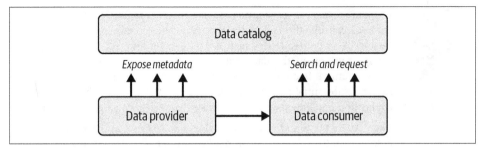

Figure 6-1. Data providers and data consumers

By which means can a data provider provide data to a data consumer? This is an important question to be able to answer before you implement a data catalog! The reality is that there are endless ways of doing that. In the following, I will describe three approaches that you can take into account:

- Centralized
- Decentralized
- Combined

The *centralized* approach uses *one* data warehouse or *one* data lake for an entire company to make data consumable. The role of the data catalog in this setup is to act as an experience layer for search on top of that one solution and to improve governance. I discuss the centralized approach in the following with the example of a data warehouse.

The *decentralized* approach uses several RDSs, APIs, and streaming technologies in each domain of the company to make data consumable. The role of the data catalog in this setup is to act as an experience layer for search across the technologies used by the domains. I discuss the decentralized approach in the following with the example of data mesh—and I take a little bit of a deep dive into this concept, to make it clear what it means.

The *combined* approach is a way to use a partly centralized, partly decentralized approach. This means that certain domains use the centralized solution to expose and share their data, while others rely on their own solutions.

For some data catalogs, solutions such as data virtualization, federation, or consolidation allow for accessing data directly in the data catalog. As a consequence, such a data catalog also becomes the storage solution of the data itself, and not only of its metadata. Keep in mind that data access directly inside the data catalog requires substantial technical work up front. It also means that the application implemented becomes more than a data catalog.

The data that is found in a data catalog and accessed in the setups described in the following must not be used for all purposes. If you are aiming at building integrations that support the operational backbone of your company, as described in Chapter 5, *do not* use the storage solutions described in the approaches in the following as part of such integrations. The use cases in the following are for analytical purposes only, such as machine learning, artificial intelligence, and business intelligence.

Let's go through the three scenarios in more depth, beginning with the centralized approach.

Centralized Approach

In the *centralized approach*, data sources from all over the company are pushed or pulled into the data catalog, and hence exposed at a metadata level in the data catalog. This goes for all approaches, but in the case of the centralized approach, the unique element is that access to requested data should not be provided directly from the provider to the consumer. Instead it goes through a central function.

In Figure 6-2, I have depicted the centralized approach to access data. In this case, the central function is a data warehouse. It could also have been a data lake or data lakehouse, or any technology or combination of technologies really, that is centrally managed and serves as the only place from which the entire company can access data.

So imagine a setup like this. All IT systems in the IT landscape (or a substantial part of them) have been pushed or pulled to the data catalog. Now, if a user searches and finds this data, they can request it. If the data is already available in the data warehouse, then the user is referred to the data warehouse where they can access the data directly. If the data is not available in the data warehouse, then the user sets up a request for that data, which triggers the owner of the data to provide it to the data warehouse for consumption.

To get data into the data warehouse is a process, an extract, transform, load (ETL) process, meaning that data must be extracted from source systems, transformed, and then loaded into the warehouse. This requires data quality work to be done up front, as the transformation of data has to both remove any irrelevant data from the data source that must not go into the data warehouse and make the data fit into the overall data structure of the data warehouse information architecture.

 This process would be a little different if the central solution was a data lake. In that case, the process of adding data to the central solution would be an extract, load, transform (ELT) process, with greater speed and less quality, unless the transformation part is actually carried out. In ELT, this task is carried out after the provider of the data has delivered the data, and therefore, the task is often considered done, because the data has been delivered to the central solution, albeit in poor quality.

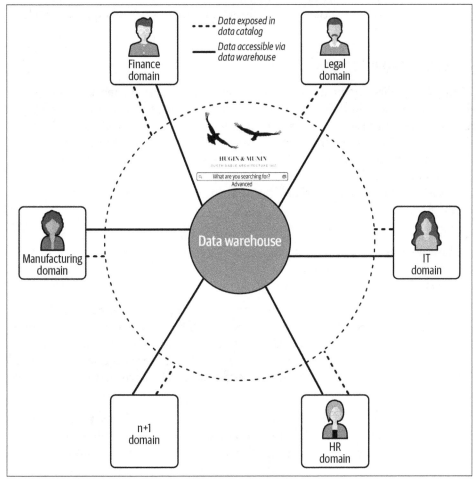

Figure 6-2. Centralized approach to access data (data warehouse)

So, what happens when you click the request button for a particular asset in a data catalog built on top of a data warehouse? Two things can happen, which are illustrated in Figure 6-2:

- You are automatically guided to the data warehouse, where the desired data is available.
- You are pushing a notification to the domain owner in the data catalog that data not yet present in the data warehouse (but discoverable in the data catalog at a metadata level) needs to be prepared and put inside the data warehouse.

As you will see next, there is general consensus that the centralized approach to accessing data is a setup of the past. Instead, the best practices in the data community are tending toward more decentralized, federated solutions.[2] This is what we will look at now.

Decentralized Approach

In the *decentralized approach,* data sources are exposed in one and the same global data catalog, just as in the case of the centralized approach. But in the decentralized approach, these data sources are made accessible via the various technologies used by the domains. This means that there is no central business unit and technology that data must be placed into in order for the data to be consumable by users who find this data in the data catalog. In the decentralized approach, there are several concepts and setups at play, such as data mesh. In the following example, I present a pragmatic data mesh setup.

Data mesh was introduced in Chapter 2, in the section "Understanding Domains." It is also important to consult the book *Data Mesh: Delivering Data-Driven Value at Scale* by Zhamak Dehghani, as she invented the term "data mesh" and presents a complete vision for a data mesh of the future.

In the context of data accessibility, a little more introduction is needed here to discuss how a data mesh enables access to data. Data mesh draws on the same metaphor as that of the World Wide Web; similar to a web, a mesh is a woven, knit, or knotted material of open texture (*https://oreil.ly/LYMl3*). A data mesh creates not a *World Wide Web,* but an *enterprise-wide web*. In a data mesh, all analytical data is searchable and accessible by default.

The need for a data mesh is rooted in scalability. Data lakes and especially data warehouses—like the one presented in the section above about the centralized approach—were conceived several decades ago. Back then, the amount of data and the need to

---

2 Certain thought leaders argue that the centralized solution is a more valid and future-proof setup, e.g., Chad Sanderson's notion of the "immutable data warehouse (*https://oreil.ly/3s-jZ*)."

access it was manageable for one, central team in a company. This is no longer the case, at least not for big, global companies. The pressure on the central data warehouse team has simply become too big; it cannot manage the amount of data that a company wants to expose and consume. It can't scale.

To allow companies to scale, they need their data architecture to be scalable. Therefore, data mesh proposes to dissolve the central data team and especially the central technology that *all* employees in the company must use to access data, like the data lake or data warehouse. Instead, data mesh suggests a domain-oriented approach, where each part of the business is responsible for exposing and making accessible their data on a data platform to the rest of the company (the data platform was discussed in Chapter 5).

Another book, *Data Management at Scale*,[3] analyzes a similar situation: a central data team, operating a company-wide data lake or data warehouse, creates a bottleneck that makes it impossible to scale as a company, to use data freely, because data cannot get from provider to consumer fast enough. And, just like Dehghani's *Data Mesh*, Strengholt's *Data Management at Scale* addresses a similar solution to this situation. There is a noteworthy difference, though. Data mesh as a concept is idealistic and looking into the future; no technology can yet completely fulfill the ambition of a data mesh, although its core is envisioned to rely on sharing data via APIs. That is not the case for the scalable data management approach, which builds on existing technologies and is more pragmatic.

Keep in mind that data mesh is a new framework and that implementing it is still both difficult and not completely supported by technology. Therefore, the following description is kept very simple in order to easily explain the data catalog in a data mesh context.

In a data mesh, the data catalog becomes as close as possible to the company equivalent of the search engine on the web. The data catalog exposes data from the domains that is consumable once discovered, as illustrated in Figure 6-3.

---

3 Piethein Strengholt, *Data Management at Scale: Best Practices for Enterprise Architecture* (Sebastopol, CA: O'Reilly, 2020) (new edition forthcoming in 2023).

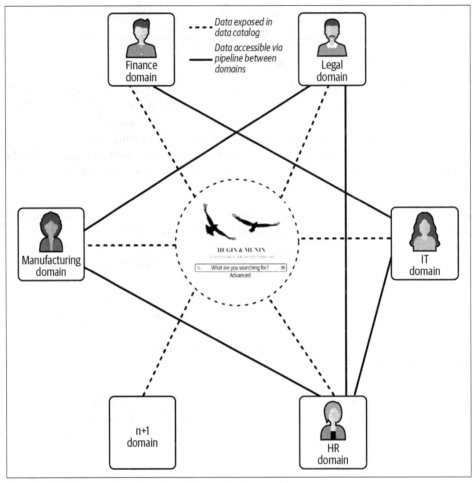

Figure 6-3. Decentralized approach to access data (data mesh)

So what happens when someone pushes the request button on an asset in a data catalog that is built on a data mesh? Two things can happen:

- In the future, a true data mesh will provide instant access to the data requested in the data catalog.[4]

---

4 As the data mesh is API-based, this will require agreed-upon standards for how to define endpoints, an understanding of how the specific endpoints could be used, and a technology to build, secure, deploy, and manage endpoints.

- In the present, a scalable data management setup will allow for data pipelines to be built directly between the provider and the consumer, bypassing a central solution that everyone has hitherto been forced to pass through. The data request is furnished, already prepared and packaged by the owning domain(s).

> If your company implements a data mesh, the data discovery team evolves into high-level consultants who ensure the overall quality of the metadata repositories needed to manage the data mesh.

Data mesh describes data *as a product*. This can be confusing when working with a data catalog, where data is defined as an asset. Nevertheless, pay attention to this distinction, as they are not alike. The general distinction is that an asset holds value and must be protected, whereas products are meant for consumption.

> Data mesh—as described by Zhamak Dehghani—is about only analytical data, not operational data. So, a data catalog can be added to the "experience layer" on top of the data mesh layer itself. But a natural consequence is two data catalogs, not one, because you would also need a data catalog of the operational data in order to govern it.

Combined Approach

In the *combined approach*, a mixed setup of centralized and decentralized approaches is used. This is the most likely scenario for data catalog implementations. Most companies find themselves in a situation that is in fact a blend of a traditional setup, with a central data warehouse that works for some parts of the company, and a decentralized setup for other parts of the company that have embarked on a more strategic, future-oriented way to share data.

With a *combined approach*, your company will have an automated access setup for certain data sources in the IT landscape. This is the data that is made accessible in the decentralized approach via one or more technologies that are controlled in the domain. Other data sources will be searchable in the data catalog and accessible via technology managed as described in the centralized approach, such as a data warehouse. Finally, certain data will be searchable in the data catalog but not accessible, as it has not yet been placed in the central data warehouse for consumption, as can be seen in Figure 6-4.

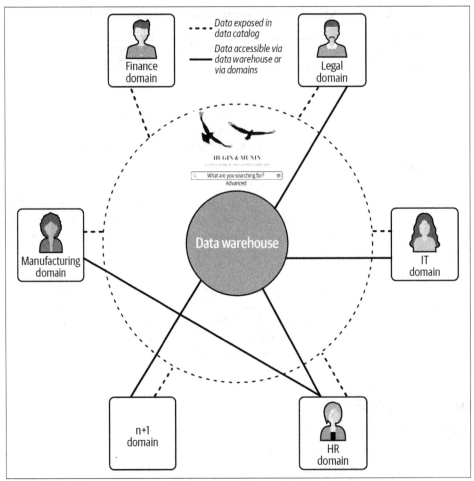

Figure 6-4. Combined approach to access data

Once you have chosen how the data in the catalog can be accessed, you need to build the domains inside your data catalog.

Building Domains

Part of implementing the data catalog involves landing your company data correctly within it. This must happen before you perform the push or pull of data sources, as I explained in Chapter 2.

Start with small steps: identify domains and subdomains; examine what data sources will go easily into the data catalog with a standard connector or via already well-defined topics in a streaming platform. This is essential if you want your data catalog to be operational and provide value. Once the data sources are represented in the data catalog, make sure to enrich the glossaries so that they can depict the assets with great specificity.

Empower end users to create domains and refine their domains on their own. You need to let the data catalog grow organically, like a strong, resilient network, without the data discovery team defining and driving forward each and every little thing within it. Allowing for autonomy builds strong, resilient networks. Minimizing interference from the data discovery team means end users have a seat at the data catalog table.

The data discovery team can empower domain owners through methodological approaches to describing their domains. This can be accomplished through questionnaires. These questionnaires are simply guidance for each domain that can ask themselves the following questions, to improve the description of the domains and the assets in the domains. I'll show you three examples of questionnaires that ask:

- Domain owners about their domain and its assets
- Asset stewards about the assets in the domain
- Asset stewards about glossary terms of the assets in the domain

Questionnaire No. 1: Domain Owner Description of Domain and Assets

In the questionnaire for domain owners, the exercise is to get them to think about their domains and how they can be described. The questionnaire might look like the one shown in Table 6-1.

Table 6-1. Questionnaire no. 1: Domain owner description of domain and assets

Choose a selection of assets from the collection to focus on, with one or only a few asset owners. It must be assets that would deliver value for many end users. Ask yourself:
What assets should we focus on and why?
How should the asset be described?
What would be the glossary terms for the asset?
Who is the steward of the assets?
Who is the owner of the assets?
What should we ask the asset owners? (The domain owner does not know all the assets in the domain.)

Questionnaire No. 2: Asset Steward Description of Assets in the Domain

In this questionnaire for asset stewards, the exercise is to get them to think about their assets and how they can be described. The questionnaire might look like the one shown in Table 6-2. Note that this questionnaire should be carried out after questionnaire no. 1.

Table 6-2. Questionnaire no. 2: Asset steward description of assets in the domain

Using the asset selection made by the domain owner in questionnaire no. 1, please answer the following questions from your perspective as an asset steward.

How would you amplify the description of the assets?
How would you assess the level of confidentiality of the assets (public, internal, etc.)?
How would you assess the level of sensitivity of the assets (non-PII, PII, etc.)?
Any other questions provided by the domain owner

Questionnaire No. 3: Asset Steward Description of the Glossary Terms of Their Assets

In questionnaire no. 3, still for asset stewards, which you can see in Table 6-3, the exercise is to establish a small contribution for the domain glossary and potentially also for the global glossary, depending on the usage of the words. Consider the answers to this questionnaire an initial contribution to the glossaries, which will gradually evolve and change over time.

Table 6-3. Questionnaire no. 3: Asset steward description of the glossary terms of their assets

Let's create the terms for the domain glossary and perhaps terms for the global glossary.

What are the terms that describe the assets in your domain?
What is the ideal name for the term?
What is the definition of the term?
Does it have an acronym?
How is the term related to other terms?
Does the term have variant terms (synonyms), and if so, what are these?
What are related terms?
Can you depict these as broader terms and narrower terms?
Are there any words that you just would like to tag your assets with? (This can also be done at a later point.)
Who knows what this is about—who is the subject-matter expert?
Who is the steward (if not the asset steward) that defines the term?

You must elaborate on these questionnaires so that they become more specific and match the exact features and structure of your company. Remember that the questionnaires are key to describing a domain and its assets—the answers to the questionnaire will improve search significantly.

Summary

In this chapter you learned key elements of implementing a data catalog:

- You should select your data catalog based on a carefully defined set of capabilities and assess data catalogs according to those capabilities.

- There will be cases where the implementation of a data catalog is in fact a catalog of catalogs. Even though this is a difficult way to implement a data catalog, it can be both a necessary and relevant approach.
- You can create access to data in three ways in a data catalog:
  - A centralized approach, which uses one global solution to make data accessible across the company
  - A decentralized approach, where each domain is capable of choosing their own solutions to make data accessible
  - A combined approach, where some data is accessible via a central solution, while certain domains in the company act more freely and have made data accessible themselves
- Questionnaires are a way to unlock the descriptions of domains and the assets in them, complete with glossary terminology.

In the next chapter, we will look at the life of data and IT systems.

CHAPTER 7

Manage Data: Improve Lifecycle Management

Imagine that you have a data catalog that has been successfully implemented. Data from data sources is gradually pushed/pulled into the data catalog, and the data catalog is being used by everyone in your organization. The data catalog is growing organically, with strong, decentralized nodes like a social network. Assets will get metadata—glossary terms, descriptions, ownership, and so on—assigned to them, and the IT landscape of your company is becoming discoverable.

Now that you have a working data catalog, you can use it to perform better data lifecycle management of the data in your IT landscape. This is a little bit of a revolution, and once you get this up and running, it will pay off. Accordingly, this chapter covers:

- Management of the lifecycle of data in the IT landscape *with* the data catalog
- Management of the lifecycles of data assets, terms, and more *in* the data catalog

At the end of this chapter, I will also discuss data observability, which will push management of data into an even earlier stage of the data lifecycle.

The Value of Data Lifecycle Management and Why the Data Catalog Is a Game Changer

In data science, computer science, data engineering, and adjacent disciplines, the *data engineering lifecycle* is well understood. This lifecycle is about getting data from source systems to serve in use cases of machine learning, business intelligence, and more. But, as pointed out in *Fundamentals of Data Engineering*,[1] the data engineering lifecycle is only one part of the entire *data lifecycle*. And managing the entire lifecycle of data at a high level is really the job of lawyers, compliance specialists, data managers, and data architects.

This chapter is about the *entire* data lifecycle. It's important because data catalogs fortunately can improve data lifecycle management substantially, with big benefits for the companies that get this.

Here's how.

Imagine being a lawyer, compliance specialist, or data architect (unless, of course, you belong to one of these professions, and you don't have to imagine it at all!). These employees fight an uphill battle trying to keep track of the data lifecycles, and it has huge consequences.

Let's consider the lawyer and compliance specialists. Part of their job is to ensure that data is kept long enough in their company. A company is forced to keep certain data for a certain period of time. The Food and Drug Administration (FDA) can require pharmaceutical companies to keep data (for example, the life of product plus 35 years) because the company must always be able to prove that its medicine only has the known, indicated side effects. If authorities like the FDA discover that the data has been deleted or lost before the retention period of that data ends, then it can issue warning letters or close production of the medicine—basically, shut down parts of a company (*https://oreil.ly/fqfLV*) or an entire company (*https://oreil.ly/LUwqE*) because it can't manage the lifecycle of its data!

And sometimes lawyers and compliance specialists must manage the data lifecycle for the opposite purpose: it *must* delete certain data after a specific period of time. The fines associated with not respecting this are very serious if authorities discover this upon inspections. For example, GDPR fines can be up to 4% of the annual global turnover of a company if a company does not delete data that should have been deleted. In 2021, Amazon was fined €746 million ($865 million) by the European Union for not adhering to GDPR because of poor data lifecycle management.

Now, let's consider a data architect. Massive data migration projects fail all the time. What data should be deleted, what should be migrated into the new system, and how? Data migration projects are often undervalued work, and those projects often end up costing a fortune.

Not managing data lifecycles correctly has regulatory, legal, and financial consequences of fatal proportions. It's serious business to be able to manage data lifecycles.

---

1 Joe Reis and Matt Housley, *Fundamentals of Data Engineering: Plan and Build Robust Data Systems* (Sebastopol, CA: O'Reilly, 2022), 37.

However, so far, the technological support for managing data lifecycles has not been great. Certain systems have existed, but most rely on manual description of data types and how to manage them from the late stages of the data lifecycle, when data was to be archived.

In this chapter, I show just how potent a game changer the data catalog is for managing the data lifecycle. For the first time ever, companies have a tool that will allow them to begin doing effective, automated data lifecycle management directly on the data in their IT landscape, via its metadata representation in the data catalog.

But not only end users of data catalogs have something to learn from this chapter. Data catalogs have, obviously, been created by computer scientists and the like. This means that not many data catalog providers have fully grasped just how efficient their technology is in gaining a better control of the entire data lifecycle—because that is not a natural focus for them.

So the providers of data catalogs, too, should read this chapter carefully.

You need to sit tight—you first need to understand lifecycles, and they can be somewhat mind-boggling!

Various Lifecycles

Think about the place where you currently work. What happened yesterday? What data did that generate? What analytical insights were extracted from that data? What decisions were made? What about one year ago, what happened back then? Five years ago? Ten? It gets harder to rely on human memory the further back in time you go. In certain cases, you need to be able to go back far in time and also preserve the data you currently work with for a distant future. Now, think about that on an enterprise scale. It's mind-boggling.

All companies, organizations, and nations are subject to laws and regulations that oblige them to remember and manage their past to varying extents. GDPR, CPRA, and similar regulations force companies to manage data for a certain period of time and in a certain way. Companies must possess a collective memory that is searchable in the future. To collect and describe all the data that constitutes a collective memory, you need a methodology and the discipline to stick to that methodology. That's where consciously managing lifecycles in a data catalog comes into play.

Lifecycles—for IT systems, for data, for glossary terms, and so on—enable the management of organizational memory. The lifecycles are, for example, manifested in data retention policies that define where data is located and how it's processed, including for how long the data must be kept.

First, let's look at the core of each lifecycle in the data catalog: the data lifecycle.

Data Lifecycle

The data lifecycle includes everything that happens in the life of data from when the data is conceived to when it is deleted. Managing the entire data lifecycle is initially done at a very high level, meaning for data objects such as employee, goods, customer order, etc. This can then be detailed further, down to specific tables in systems.

The data lifecycle has several phases, known as POSMAD,[2] as illustrated in Figure 7-1, beginning with *Plan*.

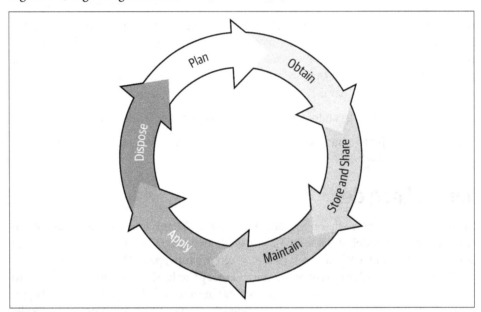

Figure 7-1. POSMAD: the data lifecycle

Let's briefly run through the various phases:

Plan

When you are developing and configuring an IT system, you must plan how to represent the data, both as a data model in conceptual, logical, and physical layers, and the data types of a given application, along with its owner, retention period, etc.

---

2 In this book, I refer to POSMAD as the data lifecycle because it effectively explains the life of data at a conceptual level, even though POSMAD was originally described as an information lifecycle. *Data* and *information* are not always perceived to be synonymous—for example, in the DIKAR model (see Chapter 8). Research on lifecycles (*https://oreil.ly/IY-Ww*) has been done, and POSMAD is found in a modified version in *Data Management Body of Knowledge* (DAMA-DMBOK), 2nd edition, 2017, p. 29.

Obtain
> This is when you obtain the data in the sense that it is captured, purchased, or created in IT systems.

Store and Share
> Once the data is in the IT system, its existence can be communicated to the rest of the organization, and users can be given access to it.

Maintain
> While the data is in the IT system, it has to be updated, changed, verified, etc. on an ongoing basis in order for the IT system to run properly.

Apply
> While the data is in the IT system, it can be used for various purposes to accomplish the organization's goals. This is the stage in which you would search for and then in data.

Dispose
> When the data is no longer needed or the retention period has expired, it must be archived or deleted from the archive. The retention period is defined by company policy.

The data lifecycle is the most central lifecycle to know, but there are others that you will encounter.

Using the Data Catalog for Data Lifecycle Management

In an organization that does not have a data catalog, if you wanted to see a complete, detailed overview of all of the data in the company, you'd only see it as part of the Dispose phase of the data lifecycle, when data is moved to long-term storage solutions and cataloged as part of that process. Without a data catalog, it is technically impossible to expose all data running in production.

Data lifecycle management is usually hard because knowledge of all data across the IT landscape is normally stored in several spreadsheets, system inventories, and other metadata repositories that provide an overview of data.

But when (and if) data in a company is to be archived,[3] it is more likely that a unified, global cataloging of data from all over the company will happen. Cataloging of data from the various IT systems from across the company is performed in the metadata repository governing the data archive—the "data catalog" of the archive. Usually, this

---

3 Technically, this is long-term data storage, not backup. Backup is about being able to restore the production environment, and the backup cycles contradict the purpose of a data archive, which is about keeping data retrievable and accessible for a distinct period of time.

is performed by one or very few teams in a company, and therefore, a global overview of data is created. It is this overview that the data catalog so powerfully pushes in the earlier phases of the data lifecycles, when data is still in production. That's why data catalogs are game changers for data lifecycle management. Instead of waiting for the Dispose phase (when you archive), the push/pull technologies of the data catalog allow you to have this overview all the way back during the Store and Share phase, as depicted in Figure 7-2.

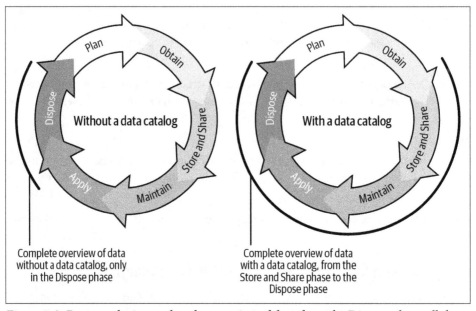

Figure 7-2. Data cataloging pushes the overview of data from the Dispose phase all the way to the Store and Share phase, providing a far earlier overview of data

That's a powerful amelioration of working with data, seen from a lifecycle perspective. Now, data from all over the IT landscape is made searchable while those systems are running in production. The data is truly becoming stored and shared, with all the many advantages that represents in terms of discovery, governance, and innovation.

To really unlock the potential of the data catalog, you have to remember that in addition to the data lifecycle, there's a data asset lifecycle as well.

The Data Asset Lifecycle in the Data Catalog

While the data lifecycle encompasses the phases in the life of data in its source, that data is represented by an asset in a data catalog, which also follows a data asset lifecycle.

If you have a clear understanding of both the data and data asset lifecycles, it allows you to properly manage both at the same time. A well-managed data asset lifecycle leads to a well-managed data lifecycle.

To properly manage data via a data catalog, you must remember that a data asset in a data catalog represents a data source at the metadata level. The metadata of that asset has a lifecycle of its own, separate from but parallel to that of the data it represents. All of these lifecycles are at play at the same time, and they are inextricably interconnected.

So, what does the data asset lifecycle look like? Figure 7-3 depicts this.

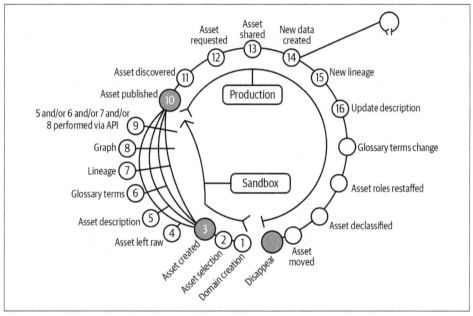

Figure 7-3. Data asset lifecycle in a data catalog

Figure 7-3 encapsulates the most substantial steps that will happen in the lifecycle of a data catalog asset. Following this will help you manage your data catalog assets by providing guidance on what to do at a given point in time. Bear in mind that Figure 7-3 shows the lifecycle of a single asset. This will never be the case, as you will most likely handle multiple assets simultaneously, and a visual representation would be a lot messier than what is depicted here.

Steps 1–9 of the data asset lifecycle take place in a "sandbox," meaning that the asset is not open for end users yet and it is still being prepared. The first steps involve creating domains, identifying the data assets that should be in the domains, and how the assets should be organized and described. This is how:

1. *Domain creation*

   Create the domain to place your data assets in. It must follow the guidance provided in Chapter 2; create your domains as either processes or capabilities, and go as wide and as deep as needed to correctly depict them in the data catalog.

2. *Asset selection*

   Identify the assets you want to place in the domain and perform the pull or push to obtain them. You will not necessarily pull or push an entire data source, and perhaps will exclude/hide views and other business logic in the source, when you select your assets.

3. *Asset created*

   You have now pulled or pushed your data sources and created your data assets in the data catalog. At this point, you must review assets for automatically detected PII—both in assets and in the data source. You should also set up additional PII rules and review/add sensitivity classification, confidentiality classification, and content classification. See Chapter 2 for details on these tasks.

After you've gone through the basic steps to get the assets into the data catalog, you now need to process them. Or not, in the case of step 4:

4. *Asset left raw*

   You can leave your assets raw, meaning that they are completely uncurated, with no owners, no glossary terms, and no descriptions. Deciding to do so will create more and more meaningless data assets. Take a look at Zipf's law in Chapter 3 again—the most frequent word will occur about twice as often as the second most frequent word, etc.

If you decide not to leave the assets raw, you can process them to add descriptions, glossary terms, lineage, and relationships. The following steps can be taken alone or simultaneously and should be performed via uploads or bulk edits. Or you can perform steps 5–8 via API, again in the combination you see fit:

5. *Asset description*

   All assets must have descriptions so that end users of the data catalog can easily understand what data the asset represents. Ideally, the asset description should explain how the data is used in its data source, as well as how it could be used in other contexts. See Chapter 2 for details on this.

6. *Glossary terms*

   All assets must be assigned glossary terms for effective retrieval. Consider both domain-specific glossary terms and global glossary terms—free glossary terms should be applicable at any point in the data asset lifecycle.

7. *Lineage*

   You must always verify that lineage is set up correctly and works. If this requires manual tasks, it should only be at an activation level that allows the data catalog's own technology to create lineage. Lineage should not be drawn by hand.

8. *Graph*

   Graph relations show how parts of an asset are linked to specific parts of other assets. This can be automatically generated/set up to be automatically generated, or done manually.

9. *Steps 5 and/or 6 and/or 7 and/or 8 performed via API*

   Most data catalogs will permit you to curate your assets using APIs. The advantage of this approach is its massivity and flexibility: you can update endless numbers of assets fast with descriptions, terms, lineage, and graph relations.

At this point, the "sandboxing" part ends and the "production" part begins:

10. *Asset published*

    The asset is published so that it is viewable for all end users in the data catalog.

11. *Asset discovered*

    If terms and descriptions have been properly added to the assets in the data catalog, the assets will be discoverable and able to be found via search by the users of the data catalog (as discussed in Chapters 3 and 4).

12. *Asset requested*

    If a user discovers an asset they'd like to use, they can then request access to the actual data that the asset represents.

13. *Asset shared*

    The data source owner grants access to the user who has requested it. Sharing data can be either a virtualization layer of data in the data catalog or to a data storage solution outside of the data catalog, depending on how sharing in your data catalog is set up, as discussed in Chapter 6.

14. *New data created*

    Once your asset has been shared, it will most likely generate new data. Once a user starts working with the requested data, the user will create a dashboard, an analysis, etc. that changes the requested data into something else—new data. That data will have a lifecycle of its own, and in the future it must create a new asset in the data catalog, once its data source is pushed/pulled.

15. *New lineage*

    The new data that is created results in a new data asset. That asset should be added downstream to the lineage of the asset from which it was created.

16. *Update description*

You may supplement the lineage diagram with an updated asset description that explains how data consumers have used the data.

Now follow a number of steps that do not have numbers because they can occur at any moment in the production part of the asset lifecycle. Consider them part of the maintenance of the data catalog, which is needed to represent the data in the IT landscape on an ongoing basis.

Glossary terms change

Over time, it's inevitable that terminology changes. For example, projects, strategies, and programs are renamed. Be aware that the lifecycle of your terms may imply that your asset should have further terminology added.

Asset roles restaffed

When people change jobs, they also leave their asset role in the catalog—for example, as owner or steward. Appointing new roles is a process you want to automate as much as possible, ideally by ensuring that your data catalog is synchronized with your Active Directory (AD). This is one of the most common reasons why data catalogs fail.

Asset declassified

Over time, assets should be declassified in terms of confidentiality, just like the NATO confidentiality classification describes, as discussed in Chapter 2. This enables data to spread further and faster to enable data-driven innovation.

Asset moved

Assets may be moved from one domain to another domain. Requests for moving assets may occur for various reasons, e.g., as a late identification of asset owner, caused by a raw crawl.

Finally, when the data asset is no longer needed, it reaches the end of its lifecycle:

Disappear

When data assets are no longer needed, they simply disappear when the push or pull does not register them anymore, because they are deleted in the source system. The data in the source system may have been migrated to a new data source in production, or it may have been exported from the data source for long-term archival storage.

As you want to keep a complete overview of your IT landscape and the data in it in your data catalog, make sure to manage this part of the lifecycle carefully. You should have push/pulls toward your data archives that would automatically depict the disappeared assets if they have been archived there.

Did you notice the parallels between the data lifecycle and the data asset lifecycle? They're quite similar. If you understand one, you can understand the other. Just remember that one describes the lifecycle of data itself, and the other describes the lifecycle of an asset (data's representation in the data catalog).

As you have seen in this section, a lot can happen in the lifecycle of a data asset. The more deliberate and thoughtful you can be about handling the asset at each step, the stronger your data catalog will become. If you set it up properly, it will enable you to manage all the data in your company. Maintain it, so that it will be kept up to date and useful. Others will find it, use it, and share it, and its usefulness will spread. But the data catalog cannot be implemented across the company at once. You cannot catalog all assets at once; you map one or a few domains at a time, starting with the most important or business-critical or the most used.

The data asset lifecycle is complicated, but it is manageable if you implement it with consistency. This is important because there are even more lifecycles within the data asset lifecycle to think about. So the better you handle the data asset lifecycle, the better you can manage the other lifecycles. Let's look at those other lifecycles next.

Glossary Term Lifecycle

The glossary term lifecycle encompasses everything that happens to a glossary term, from creation to deletion, as illustrated in Figure 7-4. The glossary term lifecycle is connected in multiple ways to data assets and their lifecycle, because terminology reflects the reasons why data was obtained in the first place, how it was applied, and the way it was disposed of (meaning if it was deleted, archived, or migrated to a new data source). A glossary term can be the name of a strategy, program, project, or virtual team in the company. It can refer to many other things that relate to what we do with data at a given point in time. Most often, glossary terms are created because new assets are pushed/pulled into the data catalog, which need terms to be described so that they are searchable.

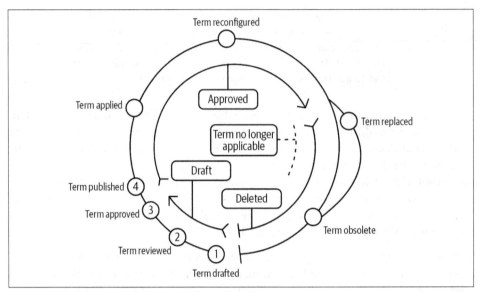

Figure 7-4. Glossary term lifecycle

Glossary terms run through a fairly simple lifecycle. At first, terms go through a draft phase:

1. *Term drafted*

   When a term for a glossary has been identified, e.g., by following the process in Chapter 6, the term is drafted with its definition and necessary components.

2. *Term reviewed*

   After the term is drafted, the term can be considered finished, at which point it must be reviewed by domain owners if the term pertains to a domain glossary or by the global glossary owner if it is a global term.

3. *Term approved*

   If the review is successfully completed, the term is approved.

After the draft phase, the term enters the approved phase, where it is put into use:

4. *Term published*

   The approved term is published and ready to be applied.

What follows are a number of application and maintenance steps that do not have numbers because they can occur multiple times:

Term applied

Users of the data catalog can find and apply the term to their assets. This is normally referred to as "tagging."

Term reconfigured

Terms can be altered in various ways after they are accepted. For example, end users could add related terms.

When a term is no longer applicable, it can enter a phase where it is replaced or deleted:

Term replaced

The term no longer accurately describes the company's data assets, and it is replaced with a term that better describes the assets. This new term goes through its own draft and approved phases, but reflects the old term in its lineage.

Term obsolete

The term no longer accurately describes the company's data assets, and it is removed from active use, to an archived state. It can no longer be applied to assets.

It is important to note that although it will no longer be possible to apply the term to an asset, the term is not actually removed from the assets it is already applied to. In this sense, a glossary term never leaves the approved phase and lives on in perpetuity because it will always be used, albeit historically.

Over time, the meaning of the free glossary terms will be lost and the uncontrolled words that are context- and people-dependent will gradually lose their search potential, as users don't understand them. Therefore, the longer the lifecycle, the more important the domain and global glossary terms become, because they ensure functional search over time.

The glossary term lifecycle is interesting because it never ends—obsolete terms are left as proof that they were used at some point. This has tremendous search implications, because you can treat it as part of tracking the data lineage of your company's terminology or the knowledge of the past in your company.

Data Source Lifecycle

The *data source lifecycle* describes the various phases of the IT systems/applications that contain your company's data—think of an ERP system with product data or a customer relationship management (CRM) system with customer data. How the data source lifecycle unfolds depends on whether it is an on-premises or cloud solution. If the software is installed on premises, i.e., on servers owned and managed by the company itself, then deployments will happen only a few times a year, whereas a DevOps approach suggests small, fast deployments, many every day, typical of cloud solutions. You can see how those lifecycles work in Figure 7-5.

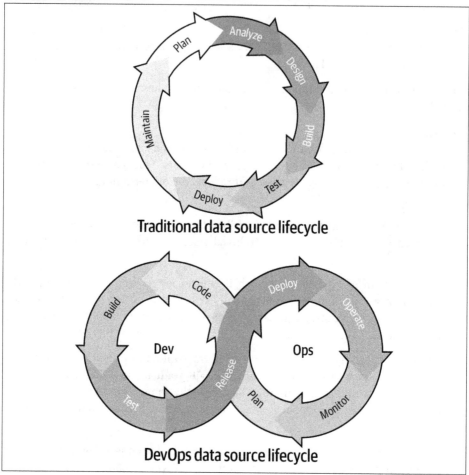

Figure 7-5. Data source lifecycles

Many changes can occur during the lifecycle of data sources: system ownership changes, scope for the data source decreases or increases, new integrations being made, and so on.[4]

---

4 Data source lifecycles are managed by, e.g., application lifecycle management (ALM) solutions, such as SAP ALM, but also more framework–based lifecycle management principles and guidelines, such as Information Technology Infrastructure Library (ITIL).

The interplay between data lifecycles and data source lifecycles is intricate and the root cause of many problems, because the lifecycle of data is longer or shorter than the lifecycle of the data source in which it resides. For example, migration of data simply happens when a data source is decommissioned.[5] In general, long-term data storage and archiving should happen continuously, so data sources have only active, used data inside them.[6]

But this interplay can be managed better and on a company-wide scale when mirrored in the data catalog. This enables a better understanding of what happens with data in the data sources—and with the data sources themselves.

 The data catalog itself is also a data source. At some point, it will be decommissioned. When this occurs, its metamodel must be archived, and its content must be migrated to a new IT system. If not, all its content is lost. Although no longer in use, the decommissioned data catalog still represents the company, at the point in time when it was decommissioned. This knowledge will have to live on in other systems and carry on the overview that the data catalog has provided.

Lifecycle Influence and Support

Lifecycles of data, data assets, data sources, and glossary terms are connected; they influence and sometimes support each other.

The lifecycles of data and data sources *influence* the lifecycles of assets and glossary terms in the data catalog, and they are themselves *supported* by the assets in the data catalog. You can see the interrelatedness of the four lifecycles in Figure 7-6.

---

5 In the first edition of the DAMA-DMBOK, the lack of management of the late stages of the data lifecycle was discussed. It has been preserved in Figure 1.2, here: "The Importance of Managing Data Assets" (*https://oreil.ly/2Mm0L*), TechTarget.

6 The ISO standards from ISO/TC 46/SC 11—Archives/Records Management (*https://oreil.ly/2daXW*) have, e.g., formalized lifecycles for long-term data storage.

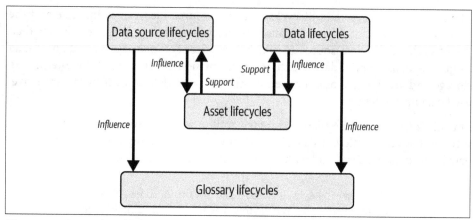

Figure 7-6. Interrelated lifecycles outside and inside data catalogs

When something happens in the lifecycle of data, then this *influences* the asset in the data catalog. Maybe a column was removed, renamed, or added to an SQL table. In a pull scenario, this will be registered when the crawler parses the data source again. In a push scenario, the streaming can synchronously update the data source—an asynchronous solution can also be put in place, but it will not be reflected in real time in the data catalog.

When something happens in the lifecycle of the asset in the data catalog, then this *supports* the data lifecycle. For example, retention times can be applied on the asset's lifecycle in the data catalog, which can trigger an alert that data needs to be deleted/considered deleted in the data source.

Glossary lifecycles are influenced by data source lifecycles and data lifecycles, as glossary terms must reflect these.

You can use lifecycles in the way you search, as we will discuss next.

Applied Search Based on Lifecycles

Lifecycles can be used as an enhancement to search. Lifecycles add a very specific dimension to search: time. For example, you could search for several assets associated with a project that has changed names, by searching for an old and a new project name. The project used to be called CRAFT, but now it is called BUILD:

```
DomainGlossary:Project CRAFT OR Project BUILD
```

You could also search for terminology back in time by looking at the glossaries and specifically searching for deleted terms:

```
GlobalGlossary:*wood* AND term status:Deleted
```

This gives an overview of how the terminology of the company has changed about all terms in the global glossary about the building material.

Imagine that Facility Management in Hugin & Munin needs to migrate data, as they are planning to decommission a larger portion of old IT systems. Due to retention policies, all confidential data must be migrated into the new system—it cannot be deleted. In such a case, it is necessary to search how much confidential data Facility Management has:

```
ClassificationOfConfidentiality:Confidential AND Capability:Facility Management
```

This returns all of the confidential assets from Facility Management. With this search result, Hugin & Munin can identify specifically what data needs to be migrated and delete the rest of the data in the IT system to be sunsetted.

Certain types of applied search will be a blend of lifecycles and compliance.

Applied Search for Regulatory Compliance

Data lifecycles vary in length because they are subject to various rules, and this defines various organizational memories. Some organizations do not need to be able to prove their actions beyond a fiscal year, but a state agency needs to document their actions for eternity so historians of the future can study the decisions of the past. Generally, three categories reflect the various degrees of memory required in an organization:

- Lightly regulated industry
- Heavily regulated industry
- Public office

Lightly regulated industries are small shops and noncomplex manufacturing companies that must adhere to things such as fiscal and privacy regulations.

Heavily regulated industries are larger corporations and complex manufacturing companies that must comply with industry-specific regulations. Some of their data must be stored, for example, for the life of a product plus 35 years.

Public offices are places such as municipal or state agencies. They are obliged to keep records of all decisions and certain data forever so that future historians are capable of studying it.

Figure 7-7 depicts the length of organizational memory of the three categories on a timeline. From the present, you should be able to go back in time and plan forward in time at various lengths, depending on the category of your organization.

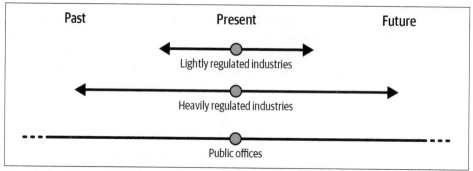

Figure 7-7. Organizational memories

Companies and public offices subject to inspections will prepare for them with audits. Auditors are employed by the company to test and prepare for real inspections carried out by the authorities. Under audits and inspections, the audit/inspection committee asks detailed questions about the IT systems that support processes and how data is treated in that regard. This is where a data catalog comes into play.

As part of a company or public office under audit or inspection, you will need to answer many very different questions from auditors or inspectors, and most likely under time pressure. Under audit and inspections, you search data and account for everything that happens in its lifecycle. You should be able to answer these questions. Can you retrieve all IT systems that support a given process? What system does what? Which data is in what system? Why? Who can access it? How is it archived? Has that been done? How is it monitored?

With proper lifecycle management of data, you will be able to answer these questions easily. Without it, you may flounder.

For example, the data protection authorities could ask HR and your DPO how the company processes the current year's employee appraisals. The appraisals are stored in a large scoring table with a column for department performance data that is not sensitive and a column that holds individual performance data that is sensitive. HR and the DPO search:

AssetType:Yearly appraisal AND ClassificationOfSensitivity:Sensitive

This returns the assets needed. Then, HR and the DPO can show the downstream lineage of those assets to the authorities. This documents how the data is processed, and Hugin & Munin can prove that they respect the data protection of their employees—their data does not end up in places where it is exposed and unprotected.

Maintenance Best Practices

As I've discussed throughout this chapter, the lifecycles of the data of your IT landscape and the lifecycles of the metadata that represents that data within your data catalog are intertwined. Not only are they complex in themselves, but their relationships with each other are as well and can be tricky to manage. Thankfully, the data catalog can help manage this.

Think of lifecycle management as a maintenance framework that is aided by the data catalog. A data catalog enables its users to understand and follow the lifecycles of data, data assets, data sources, and business terminology. This will inform you as to how you can steer the maintenance of the data in your IT landscape and how you can set up the maintenance of the associated metadata.

Let's dive into this, and look outside the data catalog first.

Maintenance of the Data Outside the Data Catalog

A data catalog can be very useful to help maintain the data in your company. To take advantage of the functionality it offers, you must integrate it into your company's data lifecycle.

As an exercise, think about how each of the data and data source lifecycle phases can be supported by the data catalog. Ask yourself: what does the phase do, and what features of the data catalog support it? Here are some examples.

Consider the Store and Share phase in the data lifecycle. What happens in this phase is that data is safely stored in repositories, which allows it to be discovered and shared on an enterprise-wide scale. Thus, a data owner stores data in a storage solution and shares it with the rest of the organization, for example by exposing it in a data catalog. Furthermore, the data owner takes into account the feasibility of the storage solution and the types of users who could access the data in the storage solution without initial approval, after having searched for and found it in the data catalog.

Consider also the Dispose phase in the data lifecycle. Here, data must be either directly deleted or archived and then, eventually, deleted. The way a data catalog can enable best practice of managing data is if the data asset in the data catalog has a retention trigger. Then, that trigger can activate the data owner and signal that the actual data—which the data assets represent—is up for deletion.

These best practices can be applied to the data source lifecycle as well. For example, decommissioning. With data properly disposed of, sunsetting an IT system is very easy from a data migration point of view, because it has been properly maintained throughout its lifecycle.

Finally, let's discuss creating or gathering new data. With the overview made possible by a data catalog, less duplicate data will be created, and therefore fewer data lifecycles need to be managed altogether, as data is made discoverable already in the Store and Share phase. This exposes data so early in its lifecycle that new, duplicate data can to some extent be avoided.

 One phase of the data lifecycle that I do not discuss in this section is the Obtain phase. This is a more rare case for data catalogs, but also very effective. If the data catalog is to engage in this phase, this is typically linked to data observability. I discuss data observability in Chapter 6 as a capability in data catalogs. Furthermore, later in this chapter you can find a discussion of how data observability enables data catalogs to push data lifecycle management from Store and Share to Obtain.

Now, let's look at the maintenance of metadata inside the data catalog.

Maintenance of Metadata Inside the Data Catalog

A data catalog must be maintained properly to stay relevant for users from across the company. Best practice of maintenance means keeping the data catalog alive as an exact mirror of the IT landscape and its data in the company. Maintenance includes managing:

- Data ownership
- Data quality
- Data uptime
- Metadata quality
- Relevance
- User adoption
- Usability

Data ownership
> Data lives longer than its owner—as people change jobs, the ownership of data changes. The data catalog needs to reflect this change in ownership in data assets, ideally in an automated fashion.

You can automate certain actions with workflow features in some data catalogs. This can help with maintenance actions such as reassigning ownership when someone leaves the company or moves internally.

Data quality

This is a difficult and somewhat subjective discipline. However, the quality of the data that is represented in the data catalog must be transparent and maintained if it decreases or increases during its lifecycle. There are tools specifically designed to do this, which can be either add-ons or part of a data catalog. Data quality metrics typically contain a rating system that ranges from, e.g., 1–3, or a label such as "nonusable" or "usable."

Data uptime

How frequently a data asset is "up and accurate."

Metadata quality

In Chapter 2, I argued that the metadata quality (the data quality of the data catalog itself) is something that should be carefully monitored, as it is a fundamental component of improving the relevance of each search performed—search relies on properly assigned glossary terms and other metadata, as specified in the Appendix. Metadata quality involves having updated data ownership, exhaustive glossary term assignment, and correct classification of content, confidentiality, and sensitivity. This ensures the continuous usefulness of the data catalog.

Relevance

This is a mechanism that must be put in place to maximize relevance in search. This mechanism may be modified by the data architects in the data discovery team and be a weighted score of search metrics, user (something is more relevant for some than for others), and serendipity—the capability to provide surprising search.

User adoption

With maintenance, the data catalog will gain significant user adoption. However, varying user adoption across the company is expressed in search behavior. If search logs reveal low activity in certain areas of the company, then the state of affairs behind this must be ascertained and improved.

Usability

If the frequency of use and data quality of an asset are high, then it's likely to be usable.

Improved Data Lifecycle Management

In the future, data catalogs will push the possibility of managing the data lifecycle to new heights. This is because it will be possible to manage the lifecycle from an even earlier point in time. I discussed how data catalogs allow us to push data lifecycle management from the Dispose phase in the data lifecycle all the way back to the Store and Share phase in the section "Using the Data Catalog for Data Lifecycle Management." This is not yet a completely integrated capability in the data catalog. However, the lifecycle capability in data catalogs will evolve even further.

Data observability is emerging as technology that aims at measuring the quality of data prior to entering solutions where data is stored and shared. This would occur during the Obtain phase, as you can see in Figure 7-8. The key benefit of this is that it turns data quality management around. It's no longer necessary to launch big, ambitious, and often failing data projects with the intention of cleaning up data after it is launched to production. Instead, data quality is monitored, and therefore it is better managed *prior* to data being stored and shared.

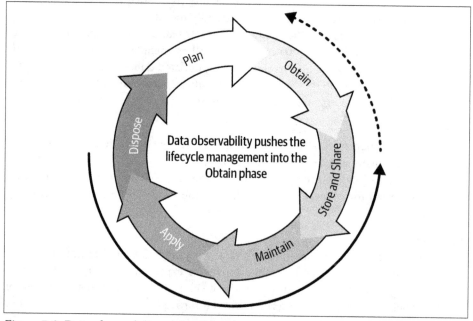

Figure 7-8. Data observability pushes lifecycle management to the Obtain phase

As of late 2022, certain vendors of data observability tools tend to mention data catalogs as a component of their solution, and not the other way around. But is a data catalog part of data observability, or is data observability part of a data catalog? This is not a debate that is settled at the time of this book's writing. But I believe data catalogs are here to stay—catalogs are millennia old and their basic functionality will remain.

However, just as for active metadata that I discussed in Chapter 5, I advise you not to focus on the technology category that vendors place themselves in, but the capability their technology performs. You should not be thinking: "What can I do with this technology?" Instead, ask yourself: "What is it I want to do with the technology I am assessing? Can it do that? Does it deliver the capabilities I want performed?"

Summary

In this chapter, I have discussed lifecycles and highlighted how lifecycles influence and support each other in a data catalog, and I showed how they can be used as a framework to maintain a data catalog as well as the data itself:

- All data in IT systems has a lifecycle. This lifecycle can be short, long, or eternal, depending on the nature of the organization it pertains to.
- The data catalog enables companies to gain a complete overview of their data earlier in the data lifecycle.
- The data catalog enables you to mirror all the data in the IT landscape of a firm, giving global control of the data lifecycle, which solves issues such as how and with whom data must be shared and when it must be deleted—or if it must not be deleted.
- The data assets inside the data catalog also have their own lifecycle, and to keep the data catalog well curated and searchable, the lifecycle of the asset must be taken into consideration when managing the assets, for example when data sources are sunsetted.
- All lifecycles—inside and outside the data catalog—are connected. Data source lifecycles and data lifecycles influence the data asset lifecycles and terminology lifecycles, whereas the two latter support the first two. You can manage your data source and your data lifecycles via the data catalog.
- Lifecycles enable applied search that takes the dimension of time into account: via lifecycles, searches can be carried out that go back in time as long as the organizational memory allows. This is the key element to be in compliance with privacy regulations and other, industry-specific regulations that require your organization to store data for a certain period of time.
- Lifecycles can be treated as a maintenance framework that can be enacted by using a data catalog.
- Data observability proposes to manage the data lifecycle in the Obtain phase, before it is stored in solutions and shared with the rest of the company.

PART III

Envisioning the Future
of Data Catalogs

In the last part of this book, I present my vision of how data catalogs will evolve in the future. In my view, they will evolve into company search engines, providing access to not only all the data but all the knowledge in your company.

In Chapter 8, "Looking Ahead: The Company Search Engine and Improved Data Management", you will take a look at the conceptual and technical foundation for a future company search engine. I will discuss how smooth and complete search in companies will be in the future.

In the Afterword, I discuss the philosophical implications of the company search engine. Just like searching the web, being able to search all the data and knowledge in your company raises many ethical dilemmas that need to be addressed and handled.

CHAPTER 8

Looking Ahead: The Company Search Engine and Improved Data Management

Throughout this book, I have discussed the capabilities of data catalogs that you can use today. You can use a data catalog so that it performs exactly as it is advertised to do and create an organized inventory of your data assets. With deliberate planning and engagement from users and stakeholders, a data catalog can permeate your company's operational habits and enrich how you work.

In this chapter, I'll take you through my thoughts on what the future has in store for data catalogs. I'll go through how data catalogs have the potential to become company search engines as I mentioned in the Preface and throughout the book. I'll share my visions with you about how data catalogs will move from being about data and orient themselves toward knowledge. Basically, I see data catalogs as having the potential to be the entry point to all of the knowledge in your company.

Here's how.

The Company Search Engine

Today, it is often the case that a company's digital assets are spread across an intranet that includes an unmanageable mix of news posts, pages of links, lists of words, strategy slides, and calendar events. Although some of the most relevant information in the company is there, it is not always easy to find. What is on the front page of that intranet and why? Not everything seems relevant. You may need to think hard when you deep dive into subpages to try to understand why data was organized in this way. It doesn't always make sense.

If we embrace the search capabilities of data catalogs, I foresee that intranets, as we know them, will fade in this decade. Intranets and data catalogs are not similar technologies, but the intranet home page that employees see when they open their browser is a crowded, inefficient place. It's packed with "useful" links to information in a structure that few familiarize themselves with because the amount of content is both overwhelming and of varying quality. I foresee that this will be replaced by a minimalist page with just your company's logo and a search bar, similar to the Hugin & Munin search bar examples I've used throughout this book. That search bar will be the first thing you see when you turn on your computer and open your browser, and it will be the gateway to everything you may need to search for during your workday. All you'd have to do is type in a word or two (or use advanced options for more complex searches, of course) to get what you need.

Are you doubtful about this evolution? If so, think back to the web of the 1990s. Back then, pages such as Yahoo.com in 1997 (*https://oreil.ly/e4GVn*) had a search bar that was weak and could not meet all the information needs of their users. The search function was supplemented with categories and subcategories for you to click through to get to the information you actually wanted. Does this sound familiar and remind you of today's intranets at all?

In the early 2000s, search engines saw a huge improvement, which resulted in the sudden collective recognition and adoption of using *search* to find what you need. Have a question about something? Google it. As I mentioned in Chapter 1, this is the reality that Peter Morville coined as ambient findability: the fact that anyone, from anywhere, can find anything. This opened patterns for human behavior hitherto unimaginable.

I foresee this as the reality that will emerge in companies. Within this decade, we will have search engines for companies, and they will be based on data catalogs. Let's look at some examples of this with our fictional company, Hugin & Munin.

The Company Search Engine in Hugin & Munin

Hugin & Munin is not just a sustainable architecture company that delivers buildings for the future. It is a company that has successfully pushed their data catalog to perform as a company search engine. There is not a single information need in Hugin & Munin that cannot be searched for.

The following searches are merely examples of a capability that will make employees significantly more productive than they are today, because everything they will be searching for is very, very close—just a search away.

Hugin & Munin has about 8,000 employees across 10 offices in Scandinavia. Each office consists of several buildings and a canteen in each building. When the employees in Hugin & Munin get hungry for lunch and want to know what's being served in the nearby canteens, they find the menus by starting to type "lunch"—just the very first letter, "l"—into the company's search engine, as you can see in Figure 8-1. The data catalog only autocompletes "l" with "unch" between 10:45 and 13:00. Outside of that time slot, "lunch" is an irrelevant search result.

Figure 8-1. Typing "l" gives access to today's menu in nearby canteens

The search provides the day's menus for the three canteens that are closest to the employee's desk location. The employees can then browse the offerings and decide which canteen to go to based on their preferences.

Let's look at another example of how information can be just one search away. In Hugin & Munin, employees must register their start time at the beginning of each day, their lunch break, and their end time. Time registration can be found by typing "tim" into the company search bar, as in Figure 8-2.

Figure 8-2. Typing "tim" gives access to the time registration system

This makes the data catalog suggest three terms, ranked by click frequency in the company. The top suggestion directs to a hit with a description of the time registration system, including a link to the system. That takes each employee directly to their current week, already filled out with codes and hours. They click confirm. Three letters, a couple of clicks. Done.

Here's another example. In Hugin & Munin, it is easy to search for a colleague. Typing the first letters of the first name of an employee makes the data catalog suggest the colleague by autocompleting the search with the full name (or full names, in case there is more than one with that name), as seen in Figure 8-3.

Figure 8-3. Typing "Gunna" provides a hit with the employee "Gunnar Asplund"

Unlike when looking people up in an org chart, this search will result in a hit that has been gathered by data from multiple sources;[1] so besides the org chart, there will be contact info, the files that the employee has created, data the employee is responsible for or knows about, business glossary terms that this person is somehow related to via projects, tasks, and so on. Also, there is a floor plan with the employee's desk, showing exactly where the person is physically. Finally, there is a chronology of the employee in the company, showing what the person has been involved in since entering the company.

Here's our next example. Hugin & Munin has a range of standardized products: furniture, interior design materials, and a series of smaller houses as second homes and cottages. One brand of cottages is called *Fritid*, which means "spare time." You can search for this product like in Figure 8-4.

---

1 This is not, e.g., an SQL job running when the end user searches—the company search engine always queries an index/graph of metadata.

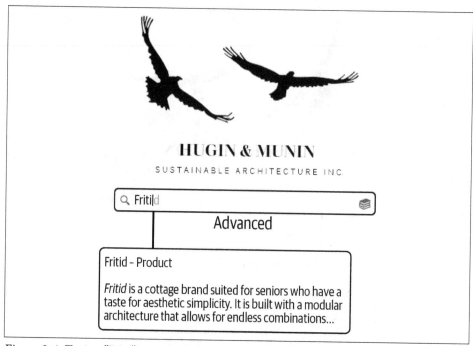

Figure 8-4. Typing "Friti" returns the product "Fritid," the series of small houses

This returns a hit with the *Fritid* cottage brand as a product. This hit includes not only the name of the product, but the description of the product, documented in the reports and drawings that ignited the series. The hit also contains analytical details about sales performance of the product across the various regions and countries of Scandinavia, present and past. It has a rich vocabulary attached to it, so that the materials in the product are nicely displayed. And the history and evolution of the product can be traced inside the hit in drawings, and the aesthetics of how the brand has evolved over time.

One final example. Employees in Hugin & Munin can search after data in 3D, as in Figure 8-5. For example, they can search for bathrooms designed with a secluded view over nature or distant rooftops, and the hits will display in 3D.

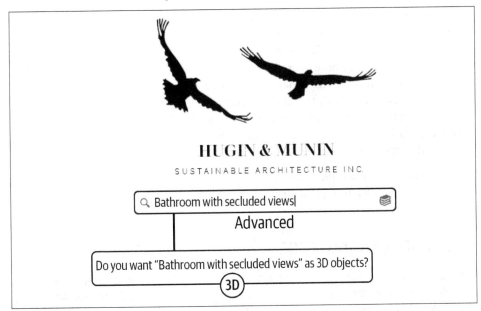

Figure 8-5. Searching in 3D

This returns hits of 3D images of bathrooms with secluded views, in all the different building styles where such bathrooms occur.

3D search already exists, just not yet in data catalogs. It is found in the pharmaceutical and petrochemical sectors, where chemicals are represented as 3D structures and are organized and searched in tools like PubChem (*https://oreil.ly/Cos45*) and ChemSpider (*https://oreil.ly/mIUmx*). In the construction sector, buildings are organized and searched in tools that allow for Building Information Modeling (*https://oreil.ly/5FigF*) like Revit (*https://oreil.ly/Oi5po*). In various industries that produce machines, vehicles, and other three-dimensional models, software such as 3Dexperience (*https://oreil.ly/PALyX*) is used to store and search data.

Data catalogs have not yet evolved into true company search engines, and not all data catalog providers would agree that they should. But as I see it, some data catalogs will evolve into search engines because of their speed and efficacy to do simple search combined with an ever-growing set of connectors that will target not only structured data (e.g., database tables), but also semistructured and unstructured data (text, videos, pictures). A search engine–like capability inside the data catalog is already a competitive parameter, and the target end state for that competition is a search engine. Not for the web, but for the company you work in.

Building a company search engine is not as easy as building search engines for the World Wide Web. Search engines for the web basically crawl markup languages, like HTML, XML, and so forth. Search engines for companies—based on an evolution of the data catalogs that we have been discussing in this book—have to crawl (or receive a stream from) a breathtaking variety of IT systems, file formats, and structures, each built in very distinct, very different ways, and placed in the cloud or on premises. It's a technical challenge, but also a potential revolution. Tech providers today work to create a smooth, frictionless feeling of data from *one* IT landscape in data catalogs, although the technical reality behind that is dizzyingly complex.

What we just discussed is not only a description of a more powerful search capability. It also represents something that makes data catalogs focus less on data and more on knowledge.

From Data to Knowledge

For data catalogs to turn into company search engines that allow employees to be capable of searching for everything, data catalogs must begin to depict the *universe of knowledge* of a given company. This includes the company's history, its people, its products, and everything else of importance.

As data catalogs evolve into the future, they will condense more data into each search hit, so that each search hit becomes a richer, more complete picture of something in a company. Basically, a search hit will no longer just display a certain type of data, but also provide additional information about what this data means in a bigger context. This is similar to the *colleague* and *product* search examples from the previous section. The search hits will not just be a name or number, but also reflect how the hit relates to other things in the company's universe of knowledge on a larger level of abstraction.

In the future, we will want more from our search results than just the data we asked for. We will want an explanation for it. We will want to ask about how data has been interpreted and what insights have been made from those interpretations. In short, we want knowledge, which is not just knowing the facts, but the ability to understand those facts in a context.

Moving from providing data to providing knowledge can be approached methodologically, with two models from LIS: DIKAR and FRBR.

The *DIKAR* (Data, Information, Knowledge, Action, and Result) model (*https://oreil.ly/bBFLO*) was presented to address that data ignites a process of human interpretation.[2] *Data* that is created in IT systems is interpreted by humans and becomes

---

2 N. Venkatraman, *Managing IT Resources as a Value Center*, IS Executive Seminar Series, Cranfield School of Management (1996).

information; understanding what that information means creates *knowledge*, upon which we can *act* to have *results*.

Following the DIKAR framework, search hits in data catalogs need to move beyond just being data interpreted as information—we need to get to a knowledge state before the data itself becomes actionable beyond the level of purely mechanical processes unleashed by events, such as payment transactions, users logging into systems, etc. Instead, this is data that has been made actionable via an interpretation of it, which has led to understanding this data as information, which again has produced knowledge. Data that has been interpreted and contextualized into knowledge holds tremendously more value than just data itself. It can spark actions that are more far-reaching than purely the mechanical/instinctive ones that the uninterpreted data itself allows for. Ask yourself: "What would it mean if I had a machine where I could search and find *knowledge*?" That would enable actions based on a deep level of reflection. All in all, as I see it, the data catalog will move away from the mechanical endeavors performed by the data engineers and toward supporting the knowledge creation of all the employees in the company. This movement is already well underway, with data catalogs reaching a wide range of users within organizations.

The *FRBR* (Functional Requirements for Bibliographic Records (*https://oreil.ly/ hC8tF*)) model is a way to qualify a more intellectually complete way of understanding not only data, but the knowledge this data is part of. FRBR has four layers:

- Work
- Expression
- Manifestation
- Item

These layers and how they relate can be described as follows:

Work is an abstraction. Think of *Fahrenheit 451*. This is a work, but, in fact, it can be many things. It can be Ray Bradbury's novel from 1953, but it can also be the movie *Fahrenheit 451*, and, in fact, it can be both François Truffaut's movie from 1966 and Ramin Bahrani's movie from 2018. When we talk about *Fahrenheit 451* conceptually as a work, we are including all these.

Expression is how the work is expressed. In our case, *Fahrenheit 451* can be expressed as a book, as a movie, as a theater play, and so on.

Manifestation is the physical manifestation of the work in a given expression. For example, the work *Fahrenheit 451* expressed as a book can manifest itself as the third edition of Ray Bradbury's book *Fahrenheit 451*.

Item is the single, physical exemplar of the manifestation—in this case, the one copy that you would hold in your hands of the third edition of Ray Bradbury's book, which is a manifestation of the work *Fahrenheit 451*, expressed as a book.

FRBR and DIKAR can help us understand how data catalogs will evolve toward knowledge in the future. As is illustrated in Figure 8-6, so far, data catalogs have operated at the three levels of FRBR below the layer *work*, and before the *Knowledge* step in DIKAR.

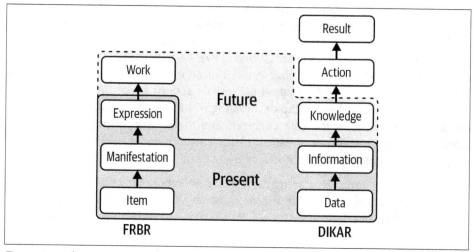

Figure 8-6. The FRBR and DIKAR models compared to present and future data catalogs

Currently, data catalogs identify data assets; for example, as a Tableau report, a table stored somewhere in a data lake, and so on. But the assets are not grouped into specific works.[3] And in the DIKAR perspective, assets are displayed before the Knowledge step. We get information about what the report contains, but not the knowledge that this gave us, and not, at all, in a bigger context of how certain parts of the business think of a given subject, wherein the report or table played a part. What mission was it part of? How did the success or failure make those employees feel? What kind of evolution did the department go through after the activities wherein the data was used? How did that make the employees in that department react? Were they promoted, did they leave the company, or were they fired? It's those kinds of questions I see an urge to dive deeper into with a company search engine.

Here is another example. Today, when we look up a colleague in a data catalog, the knowledge we can get about that person is very sparse. We might get a phone

---

3 The FRBR angle is this: the metadata representation of items equals manifestations in FRBR. The expression layer is the file format, so an asset can express itself as .json or .avro. All these layers are interpreted and become information as they are assigned glossary terms, descriptions, and so on.

number, an email. Perhaps some information about what type of data this colleague knows something about, e.g., if the person owns some data assets in that person's domain, e.g., the marketing domain. We would receive the information, based on data, that this person probably has some knowledge, but what knowledge exactly? There is a limit to what information can convey. Compare that with the more complete picture of a colleague that we discussed in the previous section. That is where data catalogs are heading! We need to think of the colleague as a *work*, in FRBR, as something very complete, and yet abstract, that can express and manifest itself in many ways. And likewise, we must think of the colleague as *Knowledge* in DIKAR, and not just bits of data we have interpreted as information. Only when we have knowledge of that colleague can we truly take action and create results. And this goes not only for colleagues, of course, but also for products, ideas, customers, and so on.

Who is going to make the choices concerning what belongs/is related to the colleague as a work? Who will define the colleague as knowledge? The company wherein the *work* and *knowledge* belong. But they will have to rely on technology that can help them with that. That, I believe, will be the company search engine.

So let me amplify my vision of the company search engine.

A Medium Theoretical Take on the Company Search Engine

The data catalog is a new technology that has led companies, for the first time ever, to have an actual overview of their data. Not just pictures in slideshows, or manually updated lists, with what are basically assumptions about the data that exists in the company. Instead, the data catalog gives the real overview. This is what data catalogs unlock. What that enables is data discovery, manifesting itself in evidence-based data governance and numerous opportunities to innovate—just as I have discussed throughout this book.

The question is then, what will the company search engine bring?

Earlier, I showed examples of how the company search engine will perform searches that discreetly change our habits and make us behave differently. We will go to different locations, where we didn't go before, in the case of lunch, because we are better informed. We act faster, as we complete cumbersome tasks more smoothly, in the case of time registration. We get a deeper understanding of the people who have worked or currently work in our companies. We will better understand the product that our companies sell, through aggregated data from multiple sources that has been compiled, interpreted, and reflected upon, and as such represents the knowledge of our company. This is what the DIKAR and FRBR frameworks contextualize.

But what are the deeper implications of the company search engine? How will it make us behave altogether? What will it make us do? How will it change companies?

To qualify this, I will introduce you to *medium theory*.

Medium theory is the study of the potential of each new medium that has been and still is being introduced into the overall ecosystem of media. Medium theory spans all of human history, studying the difference between papyrus scrolls and clay tablets as well as the difference between the pre-internet cellphones and smartphones.

In his now famous book *No Sense of Place*,[4] Joshua Meyrowitz argues that every new medium creates new behaviors and that the entire media history of human civilization can be divided into a matrix,[5] called the media matrix, that looks like this:

Orality

Orality + Literacy

Orality + Literacy + Print media

Orality + Literacy + Print media + Electronic media

Orality + Literacy + Print media + Electronic media + Digital media[6]

Every new expansion of the media matrix brings about revolutions. And every new medium inside a phase brings about a small revolution in itself.

The phase of electronic media brought about the *tele-* (distance) media, the *tele*graph, *tele*phone, and *tele*vision. Suddenly, people could write, talk, and see things over large distances. These kinds of communications were so fast and so empowering that they unleashed new behaviors. For example, the telegraph changed political decision making. Politicians on the West Coast of the United States could now be influenced instantaneously by what happened on the East Coast, and vice versa. This situation was new, and it created new behavior. Political decisions took into account a larger geographical area, faster. That changed how legislation was written and how public opinion was shaped. The telephone enabled instantaneous, intimate communication between people across continents. Television enabled coordinated audiovisual communication to millions (even tens and hundreds of millions) of viewers, simultaneously. New media not only intensifies human communication, but it also alters and expands the very way we can communicate.

---

4 Joshua Meyrowitz, *No Sense of Place: The Impact of Electronic Media on Social Behavior* (Oxford: Oxford University Press, 1985).

5 Medium theory is a field with many contributors. Meyrowitz stands on the shoulders of a long tradition of medium theorists such as Marshall McLuhan, Harold Innis, and Elizabeth Eisenstein.

6 This last phase has been added by Niels Ole Finnemann in N. O. Finnemann, "The Internet and the Emergence of a New Matrix of Media" (paper presentation, AOIR 9.0, Copenhagen, Denmark, 2008).

Likewise, digital media constitutes its own phase in media history, the one we find ourselves in, in the present. This phase comprises everything from big, mainframe computers taking up the space of entire houses in the 1950s to our current Internet of Things devices. All these digital media have changed our behaviors, giving us more ways of expressing ourselves, communicating, and coordinating human activity. Digital media has created an ever-present, increased accessibility of services that link geospatial information with basic human needs.

One of the many new media that have been introduced in the digital phase is the search engine for the web. Less than three decades ago, it wasn't common practice to search for things on the web. One had to consult a library to really get deeply informed about a subject. That is no longer the case; everything is but a couple of words and a click away. Search has become part of human practice, and the search engine as a medium has deeply changed how we behave and how we express ourselves.

The search engine has made us take for granted that we can arrive in a city in a foreign country and, without difficulty, identify places where we want to dine, shops that we want to visit, and neighborhoods we want to see. We rely on search engines when arguing with friends, family, and colleagues, when we need to fact-check something. Search engines are there for us when we can't understand the psychology behind our children's reactions, or when we are trying to fix the dishwasher. We search all the time. It's a way of expressing and acting as humans that was impossible earlier in media history.

When I think about the company search engine, I think about it in a medium theoretical light.

I imagine the company search engine as a new medium in the phase of digital media, in the media matrix. I see it as something that will expand human expression and create new behaviors. And so I ask myself: what are the truly new ways employees can express themselves with the company search engine, and what new behaviors will it create?

I have already argued that the company search engine will create a level of understanding that will push it to convey not only data and information, but knowledge. But the way I see it, the consequence of knowledge is not only to work faster, more efficiently, in a company. We rely on knowledge to act on the basis of the deepest level of reflection, and that should be embraced—but I don't see the company search engine as merely a machine to act.

I see the company search engine as the collective memory of the company it sits in; a collective memory that companies in the present do not have. Companies today suffer from a severe degree of amnesia. The cost of remembering is too high. It relies on too many full-time employees, too many manual procedures. Therefore, as time passes, companies lose their collective memory. Certain very high-level writings of the company history may exist. These are typically written to commemorate a long-time CEO or an important anniversary of the company. But the vast majority of the knowledge in companies is lost over time. It vanishes with the people who retire from the company or leave for positions outside the company.

I foresee that the company search engine will change that. The search engines on the web index the web, and therefore collective, societal knowledge. The company search engine will do the same thing for a company. The company search engine will remember, and it will answer when we ask.

What kind of behavior will that create, if employees *know* that they can find answers? How will employees change the way they work? And perhaps even more importantly, how will companies change? All in all: what are the intrinsic characteristics of the company search engine as a *medium*?

Imagine working in a company where everyone can consult the entire collective knowledge of that company without any difficulty. That's a company with no apathy. The inability to search and find the knowledge of your company, to really deep dive into why certain people made exactly the decisions they made, what made them do that, and where that brought them, that inability no longer exists. No state, no condition, is unexplainable. You will be able to know why things are the way they are, from a corporate body of knowledge that has been assembled and made searchable.

The company search engine will make companies gain self-awareness, in ways similar to how societies have gained another level of self-awareness because of the search engines of the web. The collective memory no longer resides in archives that are difficult to access, and of which the content is only displayed momentaneously, in print media like newspapers or electronic media like radio or television. The memory is ever present; it's searchable and accessible. For the company search engine, this is a self-awareness that every employee can contribute to and act upon. The company search engine makes one specific statement obsolete, namely the statement:

"I don't know."

In the future—as I see it—when it comes to corporate knowledge, we will all know. That, as you shall see in the Afterword, has philosophical implications that are both positive and negative.

But first, I will briefly discuss two questions.

Is the Company Search Engine New?

I argue that no, the company search engine is not new.

Computer historians, library and information scientists, and others may question if my vision of the company search engine is new at all. And my answer is: no—not really. Several ideas from the 20th century resemble the company search engine. Here are a few select examples.

In 1910, the Belgian entrepreneur and visionary Paul Otlet erected the *Mundaneum*, an intellectual powerhouse dedicated to cataloging the entire knowledge of the world. It used the Universal Decimal Classification (*https://oreil.ly/vdX1L*) system and had, as part of its vision, long-distance readable text from multiple sources at one time (*https://oreil.ly/tcNgU*) (website and image in French). This was an early search engine vision that could be said to bear resemblance to the company search engine, as industrial knowledge was considered part of the mission of the Mundaneum.

In the years 1939–45, Vannevar Bush put forward the papers "Mechanization and the Record" and "As We May Think," with the ambition of creating a collective memory supporting human decision making. The ideas relied on the expectation that technological progress could lead to a boom in shared searchable and accessible knowledge. Bush named his vision *memex*—short for memory expansion. This was also a vision that resembles the company search engine.

The second half of the 20th century saw the emergence of Project Xanadu, a pre-internet vision formulated by Ted Nelson. In the last part of the 20th century emerged the web and shortly thereafter the powerful search engines for the web, an obvious inspiration for suggesting a company search engine.

Accordingly, rather than suggesting that the company search engine is a new idea, I propose to think of it as a prolongation of the inherent need in human civilization to be able to store and search knowledge—a capability that has expanded remarkably with the rise of electronic and digital media.

Will the Company Search Engine Become Reality?

I foresee that yes, the company search engine will become reality.

In itself, the idea of a company search engine is actually not original, but more a natural continuation of technological visions and realizations of the 20th century. The company search engine won't constitute a revolution, but an evolution. It will be a new variant of something that has already materialized—namely, the search engine.

Technically, enabling the company search engine is much more difficult than building a search engine for the web. I discussed earlier in this chapter that the IT landscape of a company is far more complex to represent at a metadata level in a data catalog than the web is to index. And so, a "pragmatic" view would be to say that the profit motive is too small to justify the enormous task of building the search engine for companies.

But that is not the case. It will be possible to create company search engines. I suggest that data catalogs will evolve into company search engines for the following two reasons:

- An ever-growing set of connectors
- The emergence of the data platform

An ever-growing set of connectors

It is a competitive parameter for data catalog providers to create more and more connectors. It's not a matter of building a defined set of connectors, and then the job is done. It's the exact opposite: it's a race between providers to create the maximum set of connectors to the ever-growing mass of technology out there. A race is something you would want to win, and so the competitors will keep on adding connectors continuously.

This race is the first reason why data catalogs can evolve into company search engines—because connectors will decrease the complexity of representing all the data from your IT landscape, at the metadata level, in a data catalog. It's not impossible to imagine that connectors will make complete IT landscapes crawlable out of the box. That will then enable a situation where you could crawl the entire IT landscape—which is the same premise as for the search engine for the web (albeit still technically more diverse and challenging, it's doable).

The emergence of the data platform

The 2010s saw the emergence of at least three concrete proposals to create data platforms: *data fabric, data mesh,* and *scalable data management.* These theories vary in technological setup and methodology, but they are aiming for the same thing: liberating data from the operational backbone and setting it free, placing it in a self-service data platform, and exposing it, ready for consumption.

As I discussed in Chapter 5, the data platform is a strategic component in companies today. It's an area that has seen massive investments in the 2010s. And it is necessary to ask: if we extrapolate the ambition of setting data free in a data platform into the future, then what do we get? We can call it a *data marketplace,* a *mesh,* or something similar, but basically, it's a web. It's data that can be searched at a metadata level and accessed at the actual data layer.

This company web is the second—and I believe strongest—reason why we will see the emergence of the company search engine. Because if the ambitions of setting data free, by placing it on a data platform, materialize over the course of this decade, then the data infrastructure is in place to enable the company search engine. It is simply a matter of putting data on the data platform and pushing/pulling the platform into the data catalog at the metadata level, and then, there you go. That's the company search engine.

This last reason is—this is my bet—the reason why we will, by the end of this decade, witness the transformation of data catalogs into company search engines.

Summary

In this chapter I discussed the future of data catalogs and the many positive effects they will have on companies in general and data management in particular. Key take-aways include:

- You can draw parallels between data catalogs and web search engines of the 1990s in regard to search limitations and browsing supplementation. It is reasonable to expect that data catalogs will follow a similar evolution to search engines.
- The data catalog will thus evolve into a company search engine.
- Data catalogs of the future will provide ambient findability, allowing users to find everything they might need.
- In the future, data catalog search will be relied upon to carry out basic, repetitive tasks that integrate smoothly into our workday habits.
- Data catalogs will evolve from depicting just data to depicting the knowledge of your company. This will give a more complete search experience and allow for a deeper understanding of data that is more actionable.
- The company search engine can be understood via medium theory as a new medium that will expand how humans express themselves and the way they can act.
- The company search engine will create a corporate self-awareness that will make every employee knowledgeable about the past and present of their company.
- There are two main reasons why data catalogs will evolve into company search engines:
  — An ever-growing set of connectors
  — The emergence of the data platform

In the Afterword, we will discuss the dilemmas and ethical issues that arise with the company search engine.

Afterword

Throughout this book, I have put forth concepts, metrics, and methodologies that will help you improve how you implement a data catalog. I also endeavored to impress upon you the idea that how you organize your data determines how you can search for it.

In Chapter 8, I discussed the future of the data catalog and how it is likely to turn into a company search engine because it draws parallels with the evolution of the web search engine. The technology will evolve, but so will our behaviors, and that's what I want to talk about here. It's the philosophical dimension of searching for data.

The question is, what will the company search engine do to us and the places we work?

In *Ambient Findability*,[1] Peter Morville described the beginning of a new era where powerful search engines make it possible for everyone to find everything on the web from anywhere in the world. If the data is online, it can be found and used. That's ambient findability. He concluded the book with the following:

> The web has changed how we live, when we work, where we go, and what we believe. And we ain't seen nothing yet. We can glimpse what lies ahead in the eyes of a child through the lens of a Treo. A brilliant intertwingling of atoms, bits, push, pull, social, semantic, mind, and body, where what we find changes who we become. As Jorge Luis Borges promised us, in "The Garden of Forking Paths," the book and the labyrinth are one and the same. Safe travels.

I want you to remember that this was written in 2005. Morville was looking at a new reality, writing from a tipping point in time, trying to describe what he saw coming and enlighten us.

---

1 Peter Morville, *Ambient Findability: What We Find Changes Who We Become* (Sebastopol, CA: O'Reilly, 2005).

Almost 20 years have now passed since Morville wrote *Ambient Findability*. And so the question is, what happened? What did ambient findability do to us, to our civilization? How did we travel? My answer: ambient findability lets us see everything there is in the human mind, for better or for worse.

For example, ambient findability gave us the possibility to search in the entire literature in the history of humanity. Just like that. In *Uncharted: Big Data as a Lens on Human Culture*,[2] Erez Aiden and Jean-Baptiste Michel talk about their invention, Bookworm, that eventually became the Google Ngram Viewer (*https://oreil.ly/CFp--*). The Ngram Viewer is a search engine dedicated to world literature. You can search for whatever word or words you want, throughout all time in (almost) all the books in the world, and a graph will appear as the search result, with the frequency of the word over time in world literature! In their book, Aiden and Michel described what happened when they presented their prototype Bookworm to a lecture hall full of librarians:

> We had the full attention of every single person in the packed lecture hall. By the time we started showing a few examples, the energy in the room was extraordinary. Finally, after forty-five minutes, we stopped talking and booted up Bookworm. We asked the audience, "Any queries?" We were greeted with thunderous applause, the likes of which we have never heard before or since. But over it, you could hear the librarians begin to shout, unable to contain themselves: "Try *he* versus *she*!" "Type *global warming*!" "*Pirates* versus *ninjas*!" The room exploded with excitement, curiosity, glee, and utter fascination.[3]

Aiden and Michel's invention was a game changer for librarians and linguists. They could now document how words are used over time. No wonder the room of librarians was so excited.

Ambient findability provided us this light—and this is just one example of a new, positive power that has been given to our civilization in the last couple of decades by the power of search.

But there is also a dark side to ambient findability.

In *Everybody Lies: Big Data, New Data, and What the Internet Can Tell Us About Who We Really Are*,[4] Seth Stephens-Davidowitz pinpoints how search reveals us and exposes the lies we tell each other about who we want to be. One famous example that Stephens-Davidowitz discusses is the 2016 election of Donald J. Trump as president

---

2 Erez Aiden and Jean-Baptiste Michel, *Uncharted: Big Data as a Lens on Human Culture* (London: Riverhead Books, 2013).

3 Ibid., 179–80.

4 Seth Stephens-Davidowitz, *Everybody Lies: Big Data, New Data, and What the Internet Can Tell Us About Who We Really Are* (New York: HarperCollins, 2017).

of the United States. All the polls suggested that Trump wouldn't win the election. People said they wouldn't vote for him. Google searches revealed something else:

> But the major clue, I would argue, that Trump might prove a successful candidate—in the primaries, to begin with—was all that secret racism. ... The Google searches revealed a darkness and hatred among a meaningful number of Americans that pundits, for many years, missed. Search data revealed that we lived in a very different society from the one academics and journalists, relying on polls, thought that we lived in. It revealed a nasty, scary, and widespread rage that was waiting for a candidate to give voice to it.[5]

Ambient findability exposes the darkness inside us and gives it a life of its own.

Ultimately, ambient findability will find its way into companies with well-implemented data catalogs. Users will find the information they need in such a streamlined way that it will become second nature to them, and this will clear the path for discoverability, governance, and innovation. Yet what if what the user searches for is logged? In fact, what if everything that anyone will be searching for is logged? And someone, somewhere in that same company, will read those logs and analyze them. And the persons who analyze those logs will ask questions like: "What are employees searching for, and when? Why?" "How do they feel about themselves and others?" "How do they see the future of the company?"

We depict who we are when we search—even at work. And so, in the future, employee satisfaction will not be gathered with a questionnaire, but rather as metrics applied on search. We will know how employees feel and what they think, not by how they respond to standardized questions in surveys, but by how they search. We can ask ourselves: "What are the reasons for fast turnover?" "Can we identify the quiet quitters and make them stay?"

In the future, we will need to strike a fine balance between the dark and light sides of ambient findability.

Consider Implementing a Data Catalog

A closing remark: I want to encourage you to implement a data catalog in your company. I know it's a tricky technology, but the return on investment is great. Done right, a data catalog gives you a unique chance to combine the regulatory strength from data governance and compliance with the innovative power-potential of data analytics.

---

5 Ibid., 18.

In *The Phoenix Project*, a novel about IT and DevOps, the pedantic, obstruction-focused CISO at Parts Unlimited, John, lives through a personal crisis and reinvents his professional self. He delivers a career comeback that no one expected:

> John looks around as Patty, Wes, and I stare blankly at him. ... John nods and smiles broadly. He flips to the last page of the handout. "I'm proposing five things that could reduce our security-related workload by seventy-five percent." ... What he presents is breathtaking. His first proposal reduces the scope of the SOX-404 compliance program.[6]

The CISO, John, aims at performing security risk assessments that support the gradual movement toward a smoothly running IT landscape, which Parts Unlimited so badly needs to survive. He has realized that he can offer collaborative support to the most innovative parts of the business by focusing on what matters.

The point here is: John uses his overview of systems and data to focus on what matters, reduce his control paradigm, and aim it toward the most strategic, vulnerable assets. That's your data catalog, right there. It can help the CISOs and DPOs of the world to focus their energy away from being an obstructive force (which these roles only are if they are performed poorly!), toward being the vehicle of innovation.

That's why the subtitle of this book is *Improve Data Discovery, Ensure Data Governance, and Enable Innovation*. It's because it's connected. You need improved data discovery to ensure your data governance, so that it can help enable innovation.

Follow Me

Data catalogs as a technology are relatively new, but they are already impacting and changing companies as we know them. It's an exciting time for data catalogs, and new innovations are happening all the time. To keep up with the changes, join me on my website, *searchingfordata.com*. There, I will discuss news about data catalogs, provide insights regarding various features, and demo key capabilities of selected data catalogs. You will also find my newsletter, *Symphony of Search*, as well as papers, my appearances in media and at conferences, and much more.

In the Preface of this book, I mentioned that I had done my best to make this book an enjoyable, solid read. I hope you have found it to be so. You may also recall from the preface that I thanked many people who had helped me shape my ideas while this book was a manuscript. You're also welcome to shape my thinking. If you have feedback, thoughts, or ideas, please reach out to me.

See you at *searchingfordata.com*.

---

6 Gene Kim et al., *The Phoenix Project: A Novel About IT, DevOps, and Helping Your Business Win* (Portland, OR: IT Revolution Press, 2013), 270.

Data Catalog Query Language

The data catalog query language (DCQL) is not in active use in any data catalog. I have created it for this book, intended for usage in the search examples throughout the book. It is a technology-agnostic IRQL designed to create an understanding of how you search for data—while reading this book, for courses on data cataloging (check out *searchingfordata.com*), and for reference, when you practice searching with your own data catalog. With DCQL you can search in flexible ways, from small, simple search to long, complex search. As I discussed in Chapter 3, data catalogs today already use parts of DCQL-like language, but as a combination of query language commands, operators, and clickable filters—normally not as a complete, distinct query language that end users can write and execute independently of the user interface.

DCQL demonstrates the message of this book: how you organize data defines how you can search it. DCQL makes all the elements that an asset is described with searchable. And voilá: your data catalog is completely searchable in all dimensions. You can search for small groups of assets, clusters of people, relations between concepts—the possibilities are endless!

I describe the actual search commands of DCQL in Table A-1. Those are the elements that are made searchable. Table A-2 shows the Boolean operators that enable you to combine the search commands however you want. Finally, in Table A-3, you find special operators that can refine your search even more.

Table A-1. DCQL search commands

Property	Property description	Example	Assets returned by the search example
Process	All domains at all levels related to a process	Process:Recruitment	Assets in the domain(s) based on the process Recruitment
Capability	All domains at all levels related to a capability	Capability:"ReportManagement"	Assets in the domain based on the capability Report Management. For the usage of "" please see Table A-3
DomainOwner	A domain owner	DomainOwner:"Jane Jackson"	Domains with this owner
DomainSteward	A domain steward	DomainSteward:"Kris Olsson"	Domains with this steward
GenericDataSource	Data sources at the generic level without assets	GenericDataSource:"S3 bucket"	All generic data sources that are S3 buckets
SpecificDataSource	Data sources at the specific level with assets	SpecificDataSource:"S3 bucket"	All specific data sources that are S3 buckets
DataSourceOwner	A data source owner	DataSourceOwner:"John Veitch"	Data sources with this owner
AssetTypeFree	Asset type defined freely	AssetTypeFree:Picture of heartwood	Assets with the freely added definition as asset type "Picture of heartwood"
AssetTypeDefault	Asset type as defined by push or pull	AssetTypeDefault:Picture	Assets with the automatic definition as asset type Picture
FormatDefault	Format as identified in push or pull	FormatDefault:.jpg	Assets in the format of .jpg
AssetPrimaryUsage	Free description of asset usage in data source	AssetPrimaryUsage:"Metrics used for US product launch"	Assets with this exact description
AssetSecondaryUsage	Free description of potential new usages of asset	AssetSecondaryUsage:"could be used for predictive analytics"	Assets with this exact description
AssetOwner	An asset owner	AssetOwner:"Mahmoud Darwish"	Assets with this owner
AssetSteward	An asset steward	AssetSteward:"Kris Olsson"	Assets with this steward
FreeTerm	An uncontrolled term	FreeTerm:"parquet wood"	Assets with the folksonomy term "parquet wood"

Property	Property description	Example	Assets returned by the search example
DomainTerm	A domain-controlled term	DomainTerm:Ash	Assets with the taxonomy term "Ash"
GlobalTerm	A global-controlled term	GlobalTerm:"European Ash"	Assets with the ontology term "European Ash"
LineageUpstream	Lineage for asset upstream	LineageUpstream:Electricity<-"Floor plan"	Assets with upstream lineage from Floor plan to Electricity
LineageDownstream	Lineage for asset downstream	LineageDownstream:Electricity->"Floor plan"	Assets with downstream lineage from Electricity to Floor plan
GraphRelatedTo	Assets related to each other	GraphRelatedTo:Electricity>>"Floor plan"	Assets with relation between Electricity and Floor plan
ClassificationOfContent	Classification of asset content	ClassificationOfContent:*DT*	Assets pertaining to Demand Trends (DT). For the usage of ** please see Table A-3
ClassificationOfConfidentiality	Classification of asset confidentiality	ClassificationOfConfidentiality:Confidential	Assets that are Confidential
ClassificationOfSensitivity	Classification of asset sensitivity	ClassificationOfSensitivity:Sensitive	Assets that are Sensitive
CreationDate	When an asset or term was created	CreationDate:12.31.2022	Assets or terms created the 31st of December, 2022

Table A-2. DCQL Boolean operators

Operator	Visualization	Usage	Description
AND		Value 1 AND Value 2	Returns assets that hold both values
OR		Value 1 OR Value 2	Returns assets that hold one or more of the values
NOT		Value 1 NOT Value 2	Returns assets that hold value 1 and excludes those that also hold value 2
XOR		Value 1 XOR Value 2	Returns assets that hold either value 1 or value 2 but not both

Table A-3. DCQL special operators

Operator	Usage	Description
""	"Q3 2025"	Treats several words/numbers divided by blank space as one expression
()	(Value 1 OR Value 2) AND Value 3	Enhances the syntax of the search by allowing the creation of groups
*	Tree*	Returns all values beginning with the values left of the asterisk
<	<1000	Returns values smaller than
<=	<=1000	Returns values smaller than or equal to
>	>1000	Returns values greater than
>=	>=1000	Returns values greater than or equal to
->	Value 1 -> Value 2	Returns downstream lineage assets
<-	Value 1 <- Value 2	Returns upstream lineage assets
>>(n)	Value 1 >>(n) Value 2	Returns related nodes in graph n nodes away

Index

thesaurus
    broader terms (BTs), 41
    definition of term, 62
    narrower terms (NTs), 41
    preferred terms (PTs), 41
    structure of, 41
    variant terms (VTs), 41
true positive/true negative, 70 (see also confusion matrix)
Trump, Donald J., 180

U

Uncharted: Big Data as a Lens on Human Culture (Aiden and Michel), 180

usability, 155
user adoption, 101, 155

V

variant terms (VTs), 41 (see also thesaurus)
vendor analysis, 117
vendors, 118-120
vertical browsing, 66

Z

zemblanity, 76
Zipf, George Kingsley, 73
Zipf's law, 73, 90

About the Author

Ole Olesen-Bagneux holds a PhD in Information Science from the University of Copenhagen, Denmark, where he has also lectured in courses pivotal for data cataloging, such as Knowledge Organization and Information Retrieval, that teach you how to organize data in big collections and retrieve it again. He has worked within the field of Data Management and Governance as a leader, architect, and practitioner for over a decade in the life science sector. He has hands-on experience with several data catalogs, and currently works as an Enterprise Architect in GN Store Nord, in Copenhagen, Denmark.

Colophon

The animal on the cover of *The Enterprise Data Catalog* is a monarch butterfly (*Danaus plexippus*) on milkweed. Its names (both scientific and nonscientific) have several possible origins. "Monarch" could come from King William III (his secondary title was Prince of Orange) or from orange's similarity to the color of a king's crown. In Greek, its scientific name means "sleepy transformation," but its genus (*Danaus*) is also the name of Zeus's great-grandson from Greek mythology.

In appearance, monarch butterflies are iconic, with orange wings webbed with black veins and white spots on the edges. Males and females look similar, although males have two black glands on their hind wings while females have thicker black veins. Their bright colors warn predators that they are poisonous. The milkweed that monarch eggs must be laid on provides the toxin to the caterpillars when they eat the plant's leaves. Some butterflies accidentally lay their eggs on look-alike swallowwort, which poisons the caterpillars when they are born. As with other butterflies, monarchs go through the reproductive cycle of egg to caterpillar to chrysalis to butterfly.

The migratory subspecies performs a migration exceptional among insects. Most monarch butterflies live two to five weeks, but those born toward the end of the breeding season enter *diapause* (a pause in development) and migrate south from southern Canada and the northern and central United States to Mexico and Florida, despite never having migrated before. These butterflies can live six to eight months. Once spring starts at the wintering location, they lay eggs and start flying north.

The current conservation status (IUCN) of the monarch butterfly as a whole is of "Least Concern," although the migratory subspecies is "Endangered." Many of the animals on O'Reilly covers are endangered; all of them are important to the world.

The cover illustration is by Karen Montgomery, based on an antique line engraving from *Insects Abroad*. The cover fonts are Gilroy Semibold and Guardian Sans. The text font is Adobe Minion Pro; the heading font is Adobe Myriad Condensed; and the code font is Dalton Maag's Ubuntu Mono.

O'REILLY®

Learn from experts.
Become one yourself.

Books | Live online courses
Instant Answers | Virtual events
Videos | Interactive learning

Get started at oreilly.com.

CPSIA information can be obtained
at www.ICGtesting.com
Printed in the USA
JSHW070928030323
38359JS00009B/19

9 781492 098713